To: Jim & Mary.

Xmas 1998

With Love.
& Best Wishes
From
Blanche & Charlie.

Yesterday's Derby

and its Districts

THE ROD JEWELL COLLECTION

Yesterday's Derby
and its Districts

Through the lens of F.W.Scarratt

Breedon Books
Publishing Company
Derby

First published in Great Britain by
The Breedon Books Publishing Company Limited
44 Friar Gate, Derby, DE1 1DA.
1995

Dedication
To my two daughters
Kiera and Lianne

Acknowledgements
Grateful thanks are given to the following friends and
collecting colleagues for their help in compiling the data base
on F.W.Scarratt's publications: Roger Baker, Mark Brown, Biff
and Looby, Alan and Clive Champion, Dinky The MFC, John
Easter, Andrew Knighton, Roy Ling, Tom McGuinness,
Anthony Mellor, Colin Owen, Roy Scarratt, Dave Smith, John
Tomlin and Glyn Waite.
Linda Hall deserves a special mention for her patience and
diligent production of the computerised database. Also Julie
Fellows who helped with site research and providing time for
the author to write this book.
Special thanks are given to Frank Scarratt's daughter,
granddaughter and nephew for their contributions of
photographs and information.
The author would be pleased to hear of any publications to add to
the list in Appendix B.

Any of the images in this book can be purchased as a superb quality
sepia print. Please telephone 01773 852877.

ISBN 1 85983 030 7

Printed and bound by Butler & Tanner, Frome, Somerset.
Jacket printed by Premier Print of Nottingham.

Contents

Introduction

THE photographic illustrations displayed throughout this book are a representative selection from F.W.Scarratt's portfolio of bygone images of Derby and its surrounding districts.

Frank Scarratt was a local photographer of some repute, but his name was to become synonymous as Derby's first picture postcard publisher.

He was born in Allestree during 1876, and we know that when he was in his late teens he worked as a coachman for the vicar of Allestree. He was always referred to as 'Frank' instead of Francis. He came from a prolific artistic family and he produced several notable watercolour paintings between the turn of the century and the mid 1920s.

As a young man he worked as a wallpaper designer for the firm of Wilkins & Ellis of 12 St Peter's Street, Derby, a well established firm specialising in wholesale and retail paper hangings of ornate design. Their warehouse at number 12 – which belonged to Alderman Wilkins – was also a printing and bookselling 'emporium' situated approximately where McDonald's fast-food outlet is today. Wilkins & Ellis' manufactory was 'The Derby Paper Staining Works' in Brook Street, Derby (opposite Mr W.Abell's factory). They were exhibitors at the Royal Show, held at the Osmaston Park showground in July 1881.

Although Frank Scarratt was unaware of it at the time, his experience at Wilkins & Ellis would later greatly influence the style of his picture postcards, after the wallpaper and printing stationers factory was destroyed by fire, prompting him to try his luck on his own.

He started his own business around 1903, with a small shop in Boundary Road, off Uttoxeter Road, where he lived with his wife Mary, whose pet name was Polly, incidentally.

Scarratt's next move was to a small shop next door to the Vine Inn public house (Joseph Proctor was the landlord) on the corner of Abbey Street and Wilson Street, at 117 Abbey Street. In *Kelly's Directory of Derby* for 1904, Scarratt was registered here as a 'Stationer'.

Approximately two years later, in 1905, he moved to larger premises on the opposite side of the road at 114 Abbey Street, the former premises of John Simons, confectioner. It was here that he first started to take his own photographs with a

view to eventually publishing the images on picture postcards. His daughter, Winnie, confirms that his very first publication was early 1906 when she was just seven years old. Winnie worked for her father until she emigrated to Canada.

During the next five years (1906-1910) Scarratt was very active, producing approximately 400 important images of local topographical history, most of which were published by him as picture postcards.

Although Derby's other famous photographers, Richard Keene (1825-1894) and William Walter Winter (1842-1924), occasionally had their works published as postcards, neither could match Scarratt's prolific output. Scarratt's first 200 images were published as colour or tinted postcards during 1906-1908.

He gave each of his illustrations a unique number, although, despite his reputation as a perfectionist, he occasionally got it wrong. The author has been able to find only one publication below number 78. This was a coloured view of Belper River Gardens (number 17), although number 28 is alleged to be of Brookside, Breadsall. However, up to a dozen or more unnumbered early coloured views have been found and several unnumbered photographic illustrations.

All of his early illustrations were printed abroad, usually in Germany. Postcard number 100 (of Chellaston High Street) offers an insight into Scarratt's complex and time-consuming early passion for fashionable colour printing.

Photograph number 100 was sent to Karl Liebhart on 9 December 1906 for 1,000 copies off at a total price of 35s (£1.75), and received back on 20 July 1907 – nearly six months later!

This valuable piece of information was pencilled by Scarratt on the reverse side and clearly shows that Germany had printing techniques that were not available in the UK. Scarratt published several tinted postcards – a sort of single colour wash over the whole image – and green, brown and blue prints have been found.

However, the novelty of coloured/tinted illustrations did not last long, as the demand for real photographic illustrations became more fashionable.

During Scarratt's next three years (1908-10) at his Abbey Street premises he published approximately a further 200 images, mainly black

Francis William Scarratt and wife, Mary, pictured in about 1905, when he was in his late 20s. The photograph was taken by one of his competitors, Frederick J.Boyes of 22 Osmaston Road, Derby, who was a silver and gold medalist photographer (1888-1925).

and white or sepia-toned real photographs. The bulk of this output came from late 1908 to the middle of 1910.

Most of Scarratt's early photographic postcards were published as black and white images surrounded by a plain white border.

However, the knowledge and skill he had gained as a wallpaper designer at Wilkins & Ellis', coupled with his own artistic talent, soon brought about changes to his publications. The vast majority of Scarratt's next 700 or so postcards contained the photographic image surrounded by

a variety of ornate framed borders. Some were ovals, palettes and scrolls and up to 16 different types are recorded (see Appendix A).

Numbers 216-383 were produced at Abbey Street, but at some time in 1910, Frank Scarratt uprooted his family once more and moved to 115 Normanton Road, Derby, situated on the short stretch between Melbourne Street (nearest) and Hartington Street, next door to William Harty's

tailor's shop.

Around the next 700 of his postcards were published here (numbers 392-1100 approximately) from about 1910 to 1917. However, he additionally acquired his large prestigious new premises in Derby Market Hall during the same year of 1910. Some of the cards (but not many) have reference to being published from the Market Hall, rather than Normanton Road.

His Market Hall postcard publishing business was situated on the balcony to the right of the famous Market Hall clock as one climbed the stairs, as seen in the *c.*1915 interior photograph (below).

Several of Scarratt's photographs were published in the *Derby Evening Telegraph* between 1908 and the early 1930s.

When Frank started in the postcard wholesale business, he travelled around on a carrier bike to visit customers with his samples and to take photographs. For longer journeys he would hire a pony and trap.

During the period 1906-1914, Frank would set off on his bicycle to capture places of interest

F.W.Scarratt's postcard publishing business situated on the balcony of Derby Market Hall about 1915, to the right of the famous Market Hall clock and steps. From 1910, Derby folk bought their local images from Scarratt's prestigious stall.

through his camera lens. Later he acquired a Douglas belt-driven motor bike for his photographic missions.

One of the unique features of Scarratt's photography was his intentional positioning of both his carrier bike or motor bike such that they feature in most of his postcard illustrations.

The other feature was to include members of his own family in the photographs. Throughout the book his wife Mary, daughter Winnie, son Alec and brothers Thomas and Albert are often featured in the photographs. On some of Scarratt's journeys around Derby and districts he had a travelling companion. An unknown business acquaintance from Wildt & Kray, the famous birthday and greetings card publishers. This person can be seen on several of Scarratt's photographs usually on his motor bike.

Scarratt used to sell a wide variety of Wildt & Kray greeting cards as well as his own photographic postcards.

At some time in late 1920s, Scarratt purchased a Bullnose Morris Cowley two-seater motor car complete with dicky seat at the back. No doubt this was more comfortable for his wife Mary when she accompanied her nomadic husband on his travels. The car is featured in but a few of his photographs in this book.

The last 750 or so photographs (numbers 1101-1846 approximately) produced by Scarratt were all published from his Derby Market Hall premises in the period 1917-1938.

Frank and Mary eventually left Normanton Road and took up residence in North Avenue, Mickleover, in the mid-1920s. This was to be their home for the next 40 years. The Market Hall business continued, but photographic postcards with numbers above 1540 were published from '39 Cavendish entrance, Market Hall, Derby'.

We know that he left the Market Hall in c.1932, probably at the time when the balcony stalls were being shut down. He opened new premises in Lock Up Yard near the Tiger Bar and traded here until selling the business to his son-in-law, Edwin White, in c.1938. Edwin continued trading in postcards and greetings cards until c.1945. After the war Edwin had premises in St James's Chambers.

Scarratt occasionally produced photographic postcards that initially appear to be attributed to other people, mainly Post Offices (eg numbers 820/821 for B.A.Sidley, St Dunstan's Post Office, Osmaston Road; S.Wragg, Post Office, Castle Donington; Stapleton Post Office; Duffield, etc.).

Some mysteries still prevail, though. For instance, postcard number 1287 of Elvaston

Castle Gardens by F.W.Scarratt, 28 Green Lane, Derby. This is only the third card from this address ever to be found. And postcard numbers 908-909 (of Chellaston) are by F.W.Scarratt & Co Publishers, 77 & 115 Normanton Road, Derby – again, the only cards found so far to mention number 77.

During his prolific reign he visited and captured the images of most of the churches in Derby, Derbyshire and other surrounding districts.

He was a member of the Derby Sketching Club and exhibited his work on many occasions. Some of his paintings were sold in America, whilst others are treasured by his surviving family.

Scarratt was a very strict person and old fashioned in his ways and values. He thought that 'little children should only be seen and not heard', especially when playing football outside his house. Scarratt would never set foot in Woolworth stores because they were not British, and would refuse to buy a box of matches unless they were England's Glory.

Frank Scarratt was an expert in the art of copperplate writing and scorned the use of fountain and ball-point pens. He would use only the old fashioned school 'scratch pen' with reusable nib. His hand can be witnessed in photographs 944, 945, 975, 968. I am sure he would have difficulty with the way of the world of the mid-1990s

From an early age his brother, Albert was extremely interested in both two and four-wheeled vehicles and he opened a 'practical cycle repair business' at 75 Peet Street where Albert built his cycles and repaired cars in a workshop situated at the bottom of the garden.

75, PEET STREET,
DERBY

M   19

Dr. to A. C. SCARRATT
PRACTICAL CYCLE BUILDER & REPAIRER, ENAMELLING.
MOTOR REPAIRS, OVERHAULS, REBUSHING,
BRAZING, TURNING, ETC.

BUILT BY
A.C. SCARRATT
THE PEET CYCLE
PEET ST.
DERBY.

F.W.Scarratt's brother Albert at the wheel of CH-240 in Evans' Garage, Friar Gate, Derby.

Frank and Albert Scarratt's father, Thomas Scarratt, who lived nearby on the other side of the archway at 79 Peet Street, was for many years the proprietor of a horse-drawn cab. The archway between numbers 75 and 79 led down to the stables where Thomas kept his horses and cab. He regularly worked out of the LMS Station, Derby.

Francis William Scarratt was born in 1876 and married Mary in 1897 at the tender age of 21. He retired in 1938, selling the business to his daughter Winnie and her husband. His wife Mary died in 1959, two years after their diamond wedding anniversary. Frank died on 29 March 1964, at the age of 88, having lived at 13 North Avenue, Mickleover, for over 40 years. He was a member of the Mickleover OAP Association and All Saints' Church, Mickleover.

Unfortunately, after his death Frank's old and important cameras and equipment together with thousands of photographs, negatives and postcards were thrown away. Thus the old postcards in circulation today are the only source of this important photographer's work, making his postcards scarce historical documents in terms of

Frank Scarratt and his wife Mary in the garden of their Mickleover home in the 1950s.

F.W. Scarratt and his wife, pictured right, at the wedding of their second daughter Annie.

Frank Scarratt, photographed some four years before his death, with Mary, the daughter of his nephew, Roy. Note some of Frank's paintings hanging on the wall. Frank gave advice to the talented Mary, who has produced several works herself, thus continuing the artistic family tradition of the Scarratts.

topographical history (and a good investment, too).

Frank descended from a long line of Scarratts, so far traced back to 1771. As well as his two brothers, Albert and Thomas (featured in some of his work), he had two sisters, Florence and Rose Ellen. Frank's youngest daughter Annie unfortunately died in her early 20s due to pneumonia. However, his eldest daughter Winnie survives at 97 and lives with her daughter Bettie Davis in Berry Narbor, Ilfracombe in North Devon. His other granddaughter Eileen (his son Alec's daughter) lives in Stourbridge and his nephew Roy (brother Albert's son) in Mickleover, Derby. The author hopes that Frank Scarratt's remaining family are pleased with this definitive work on their talented relation.

He was, indeed, the pioneer of postcard publishing in Derby and his 1,846 recorded photographic images are a rich source of topographical information for local historians and collectors. He took his work to the people, travelling many miles to capture local places of interest and in return offering them for sale so that people could send local records of their street or village to family and friends. His devotion to photography and his endeavours in recording local scenes over many years make him one of the most important people in Derby's recent history.

Scarratt's Town Scenes

Albert Street. Young and old find time for a stroll and to compose themselves for Scarratt's *c.*1909 photograph. The culverting of Markeaton Brook east of St Peter's Bridge was completed in 1840, the street being named after Queen Victoria's husband. J.W.Simpson & Sons' printing works are on the left, before moving later to Friar Gate. At this time Albert Street boasted three public houses. The large globe bracket lamp on the immediate left advertises the Central of Cox & Gerrard Ltd. Just beyond the striped awning of Cooper & Co grocers is the bracket lamp of the Albert Vaults, run by Criss Tinley. The W.E.Burrows horse-drawn vehicle to the right has just made a delivery to the Castle Vaults (globe lamp). The striped barber's pole of George Thomas Stevenson is visible in the distant left. The Palace Theatre of Varieties opened in 1897 and Derby people were able to see the likes of Dan Leno, G.H.Elliot and, allegedly, Charlie Chaplin, before it closed in 1914 due to the success of the Hippodrome. This former Corn Exchange building of 1862 had a variety of uses – Palais De Danse in 1919, *Derby Evening Telegraph* offices in 1929 and today a snooker club, travel centre and sports shop etc. *FWS 333*

Becket Street. Children standing near an old gas lamp on the corner of Bramble Street, with penny-farthing style pram *c.*1907-08, and a man pulling a handcart with passengers on board. The Free Library and Museum clock tower is clearly visible on The Wardwick, with the Jacobean House on the top right. The Borough Education offices (Local Board) are situated here, opened October 1893 (now Berlin's 'fun pub') This coloured card was also issued earlier as a black and white postcard number 205. *FWS 591*

Cheapside. A mid-1920s view from The Wardwick of the bus terminus. Bus registration number CH 418L is parked outside the corner railings of St Werburgh's Church. As now, only four shops existed on the north side. The building with the advertisements housed Robert Howitt's, the boot maker, who existed here for many years (now Gormans shoe shop). The barber's pole on the distant south side is that of A.Birchall's hairdressing shop. *FWS 1180*

Corn Market. The open-top tram passing H.Samuels famous clock on its way to the Market Place *c.*1910. Two Boy Scouts holding lifeboat collection boxes await donations alongside the hansom cab 'taxi' rank. The black and white half-timbered building on the right is the Old Angel Inn standing next to the Maypole Dairy Co shop. The adjacent shop advertising the 'largest and cheapest tobacconist in the world' is that of Salmon & Gluckstein Ltd. The large pedimented building top right is the former town house of the Duke of Devonshire (built 1750). Much of this area was drastically modernised in the 1960s. *FWS 332*

Cornmarket. A busy scene in the mid-1930s with a variety of vehicles in view. LMS horse-drawn cart number 3308, single-decker bus registration number RC 2346 and trolley bus advertising The Tiger lounge and bars. Many of Derby's well-known shops appeared on the right-hand side in the lower portion of the large 1750s town house. On the east side are Thomas Smithards butcher's, then Spalls with Horace E.Ramsden's restaurant at number 35. On the west side are Bourne & Hussey outfitters, Jas. Moore watchmakers, and then the Christian Science Reading Room. *FWS 1668*

Derby from the river. A tranquil *c.*1915 view taken from the old Exeter Bridge, showing the various flourishing industrial sites existing on the side of the River Derwent, which was navigable at this point. The famous Silk Mill, the first factory in England, dating from 1702 and engineered by George Sorocold (who gave Derby its first piped water) is at the top right. The mill was built on an island in the Derwent and was originally five stories high with 468 windows. It was largely destroyed by fire in 1910, but rebuilt with only three stories including the famous tower. It now houses Derby's Industrial Museum. Various tanneries existed on the left. *FWS 980*

Exeter Bridge, Derwent Street. A *c.*1932 view of the new Exeter Bridge. After widening and reconstruction in 1931, it was officially opened by Herbert Morrison, Minister of Transport. The Silk Mill Tower and Power Station can be seen, together with the twin towers of Graham & Bennett's timber yard on the right. *FWS 1576*

Green Lane. Looking from Normanton Road towards Victoria Street with All Saints' Church tower in the distant left. Edwardian children linger in the upper portion of Green Lane *c.*1908-09 with Wilson Street to the left. *FWS 240*

The Grand Theatre. Situated on Babington Lane. Taken from Gower Street (anciently called Blood Lane) *c.*1912, Scarratt has captured the fine Italian Renaissance style of Derby's Opera House and Grand Theatre. It was designed by Oliver Essex for A.Melville in 1886 at a cost of £20,000. In the mayor's opening speech he declared the building to be fireproof. Alas, it was all but destroyed by fire some six weeks later. The interior was in three tiers: lower pit and pit stalls; second floor, dress circle and private boxes; upper floor, the gallery. In all the theatre could seat 2,500 people. Originally there were nine pairs of double doors allowing entrance to the above. The building is now Eclipse, part of Derby's night club scene. The wall on the right was that of the grounds of Abbott's Hill House. The confectionery shop of Edward Chattell's was situated to the left. The buildings on the left were the former Council Offices. *FWS 621*

The Hippodrome, Green Lane. A *c.*1915 view looking towards Victoria Street, with a young lady in straw boater studying the Hippodrome's latest advertising poster. The corner shop at the junction with Macklin Street is that of Thomas Glover, tobacconist, at 62 Green Lane. Further down the enamelled advertising signs apply to James Shardlow's newsagent's shop at number 54. The wall on the right hides the elegant Regency residence of notable surgeon and physician Dr George Sims (demolished in 1925). *FWS 976*

The Hippodrome. A close-up photograph taken from the corner of St Peter's Churchyard in *c.*1915. The Hippodrome was a popular music hall when opened in 1913. It was designed by Alexander MacPherson of Derby. To the right lies Macklin Street. The advertising hoardings dated Monday, 17 August advertise the latest attractions. 'The famous Craggs', Jack Straw, Alice Carver & Co and others. They would appear twice nightly at 6.50pm and 9.00pm with prices at 3d and 1s 6d. The impact of the cinema and later television reduced the Hippodrome theatre to a less glamorous bingo hall. *FWS 977*

All Saints' Church, The Consistory. An enclosed space with a high canopied seat and desks dating from 1634, this was situated in the north aisle of All Saints'. Scarratt has captured the fine works of art and various magnificent memorials in his *c.*1914 interior photograph. *FWS 849*

All Saints' Church, Irongate. The church was designed by James Gibbs in association with builder Francis Smith. Originally a tenth-century church, it was demolished in 1723, although the tower dating from the time of Henry VIII was retained. This *c.*1911 view shows how the 212ft high tower dominates Irongate. The new Tudor style cladding added to the Dolphin public house, which dates from *c.*1530, can be seen on the corner of Full Street. In 1927, All Saints' became Derby Cathedral. *FWS 504*

All Saints' Church. This interior *c*.1916 view shows the beautiful screen of rich open ironwork by Robert Bakewell which cost £500.It was reseated in 1874-75, and completely restored in 1905 at a cost of £10,000, affording 1,500 sittings. The Church of All Saints' or All Hallows was one of the two collegiate churches of Derby in the time of Edward the Confessor. The church contained many ornate memorials and monuments – *eg* Bess of Hardwick, Joseph Pickford, George Moneypenny, William 2nd Earl of Devonshire, Colonel Charles Cavendish and Henry Cavendish – many of which were created by Derby man John Smithson. *FWS 848*

St James's Street. After the culverting of Markeaton Brook at St James's Bridge, this elegant shopping thoroughfare was created in 1863. Early motor vehicle registration number R55 is approaching the St James's Hotel on the left. This *c*.1914 view looking towards the Corn Market shows George Thomas Lowe's confectioner's shop on the left (cycle parked) with John Riches draper's shop just beyond the St James's Vaults. On the immediate right are John Innes & Sons estate agents at number 24. The row of hanging lamps further up belong to J.V.Woodward & Son watchmakers and opticians, who had connections with John Whitehurst (this was also issued by Scarratt as sepia photograph postcard 598). *FWS 1060*

The Long Bridge and Weir. The wooden long bridge over the River Derwent was one of Derby's famous landmarks and was originally built as a towpath for horses drawing barges along the Derby Canal, and later used as a footpath after the demise of the canal. The bridge was 100 yards long and was closed in 1950 before being demolished in 1959. This *c.*1910 view shows another of Derby's landmarks, the Shot Tower in the left background. The Guildhall clock tower and Market Hall are also visible in the distance. *FWS 327*

The Town Hall. The Guildhall designed by Henry Duesbury in 1842 after the destruction by fire of an earlier building in 1841. This busy scene with open-top tram, cycles and carts, was taken mid-afternoon in 1911. The Shot Tower is visible behind the Police Station. The statue of M.T.Bass, brewer and great benefactor of Derby, stands on the Market Place in front of the *Derbyshire Advertiser* offices and Frost's the butcher's is to the right of the Guildhall. The statue, sculpted by Sir J.E.Boehm, was unveiled in 1885 and resited near the Museum in 1925, as it was considered to be a hindrance to traffic, part of Market Head and Cornmarket rewidening scheme. The statue is now in Museum Square. *FWS 506*

Market Hall. The covered Market Hall was designed by Borough architect and surveyor Thorburn in 1864 and was opened on 29 May 1866 with a gala concert where massed choirs sang the *Messiah*. The roof was formed by iron ribs of a single span covering an area 220ft x 110ft. The iron was cast at J. & G.Haywood's Phoenix Foundry on Phoenix Street. The famous market clock was a turret type made in *c*.1870s by Edward Johnson, the St Peter's Street clockmaker and jeweller (removed in 1988). This busy *c*.1914 midday scene shows the stalls without canopies. On the right George Hunt's ironmonger stall advertises, 'Best prices given for horses hair'. J.Cohen's fancy goods and Seaton's toffee stall are in the foreground. Scarratt's own stall is on the balcony. The balcony stalls were dispensed with in the 1930s. The author, together with his two daughters, used to run a successful sepia print and postcard stall on the balcony near the cafe from 1991-1993 until the 'Market Mafia' closed it down. *FWS 847*

Market Place, War Memorial. Situated in a prominent position in the Market Place and originally to remember those Derby people who died in World War One, the War Memorial was designed by C.A.Thompson and the sculpter was A.G.Walker A.R.A, both local men. This scene was taken in *c*.1927, with the new premises of Barlow & Taylors on the corner of Irongate (completed in 1925). To the right stands the Old Wine Vaults public house. The memorial was unveiled on 11 November 1924 by Alderman Oswald Ling who inaugurated the project as mayor in 1922. The band of the 5th Battalion Sherwood Foresters played selections on the day of the ceremony. *FWS 1308*

Market Place, War Memorial. An unusual Scarratt photograph of the War Memorial taken from the Guildhall archway shortly after its birth, with the ugly Market Head buildings (including Carters china shop) awaiting demolition. It commenced October 1924 to make way for Barlow & Taylors new drapery premises. This photograph was featured by the *Derby Evening Telegraph. FWS 1181*

St Alkmund's Church. The ninth-century church was pulled down in 1841 and rebuilt in 1846 at a cost of £12,000. It was of the decorated style, by Derby architect Henry Stevens. The pinnacled western tower supported a conspicuous lofty octagonal spire 216ft high. It was demolished in 1967 as part of the Inner Ring Road scheme which destroyed the beautiful St Alkmund's Churchyard, a Georgian oasis in the city. In this superb 1907 view the open-top electric tram car number 14 has just passed the Eagle and Child home brew public house. The premises of Smith & Sons clockmakers are on the top left corner with King Street, with the twin bracket lamps advertising the Acorn Hotel adjacent. This was previously the home of John Whitehurst FRS (1713-1788), Derby's eminent clockmaker. Many of the buildings on the left were demolished for road widening and, in 1932, for the building of the Queen Street Swimming Baths. *Issued as unnumbered colour postcard.*

St Alkmund's Church interior. This *c.*1914 view shows the handsome east window with its five lights with pointed arches and flowing tracery. (Description from *Derby Churches Old and New* by C.J.Payne, 1893). Note the beautiful carved stone pulpit fixed to the chancel arch south pier (right). The eagle lectern on the left was made of wood. Derby's eminent painter Joseph Wright – 'Wright of Derby' – was born in the town in 1734 and was buried at St Alkmund's. Memorials also existed to the Gisbourne family. *FWS 834*

Queen Street. This early unnumbered coloured publication of 1906-07 is from the top of Irongate looking towards St Alkmund's Church. Mrs Sarah Jane Bennett's saddlers shop is on the left (west) at number 49, with Alfred Blood's tobacconist shop next door. To the right was All Saints' sub-Post Office, with the Bull's Head public house further up on the east side.

St Peter's Church from Churchyard. The gentleman in the straw boater hat enjoys the sunshine in St Peter's Churchyard *c.*1914. The old Derby Free Grammar School (*c.*1600) can be seen behind the trees and is now the Derby Heritage Centre (1993). St Peter's Church dates back to the eleventh century but was restored and extended during the period 1896-1900. This photograph of Scarratt's was featured in the *Derby Evening Telegraph. FWS 846*

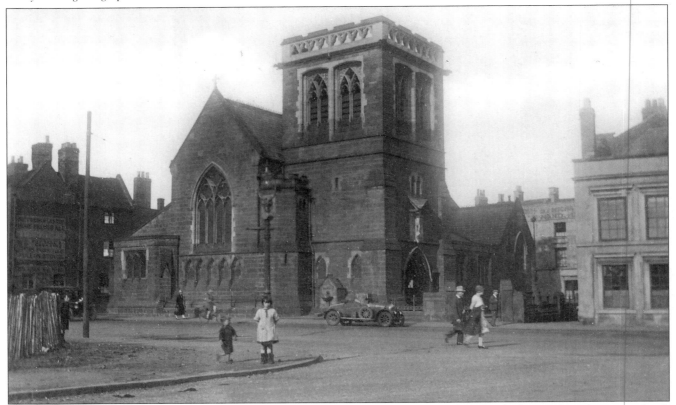

St Michael's Church. The new St Michael's Church, shown here in *c.*1927, was reopened in 1858 after the former eleventh-century church collapsed on 17 August 1856. It has a noticeable squat tower at the west end of the south aisle. This replacement was designed by H.I.Stevens, but was deconsecrated in 1978, becoming an architects' office in 1985. In this view, taken from the top of Walker Lane, one can see Scarratt's Bullnose Morris parked adjacent to the church. Over the church entrance is a memorial to those who died in World War One. The building on the right is part of the seventeenth-century St Michael's House, next to which stood the Bull's Head Inn. Unaccompanied toddlers felt safe to roam the town in those days. *FWS 1311*

King Street, Derby. This is an extremely scarce *c.*1927 photograph of King Street taken from the vicinity of St Helen's Street looking towards Queen Street. On the bottom right (south side) is the Offilers Ales New Flower Pot public house standing on the corner of Chapel Street. On the opposite corner are the iron railings of the Wesleyan Methodist Chapel. Behind the large lamp standard stood the well established butcher's premises of Albert Dunnicliffe. On the left (north side) are the two awnings belonging to Jas. E. Yeomans house furnishers. The open-top motor vehicle parked next door has probably paid a visit to the former motor engineers and garage of A.R. Atkey & Co. *FWS 1330*

River Gardens. These gardens were laid out and opened to the public during the early part of 1934 as part of the Central Improvements Scheme. They consisted of two acres of gardens and river walks below Exeter Bridge. There were three entrances, Corporation Street, Exeter Bridge and the Central Bus Station. The well-laid out dahlia garden was a significant place of interest in this *c.*1936 view. The new Exeter Bridge (1931) is in the background. *FWS 1710*

River Gardens. A bowler hatted gentleman smokes his pipe in a peaceful and extremely tidy part of the River Gardens. This *c.*1935 photograph was taken from a position further back from the previous picture alongside the lengthy dahlia gardens. Scarratt's car is parked up near the fence looking towards Exeter Bridge. This is a private photograph of Scarratt's (not a postcard) and is personally signed 'with compliments F.W.Scarratt'.

Sadler Gate. The flood water rose outside the Half Moon public house in Sadler Gate on Sunday morning, 22 May 1932. Scarratt must have had his wellington boots on for this photograph. Next door was Percy Battie's hosiery and outfitters shop – did you get your school uniform from here? This family business at 29 Sadler Gate is still going strong today. The small parking sign outside the Half Moon's arched entrance states. 'Time limit 15 minutes', whilst the pub sign advertises Maltanop fine ales. Further up on the right just beyond the Strand Arcade are Dewhursts the butcher's and Hunters the tea stockists. *FWS 1587*

Queen Victoria's Statue. This was situated near The Spot in front of Freeman, Hardy & Willis's shoe shop at the junction of Osmaston and London Roads in 1906. The statue by C.B.Birch was of bronze on a granite pedestal, being presented by Derby's famous engineer Sir Alfred Searle Haslam. The statue was unveiled by King Edward VII on 28 June 1906, whilst in Derby for the Royal Show in Osmaston Park. It was resited to the grounds of the Derbyshire Royal Infirmary in 1928. *FWS 97*

The Spot. The rear of Queen Victoria's statue dominates the upper portion of St Peter Street – popularly known as The Spot – in this scene *c.1913*. The double gabled half-timbered black and white building on the left with four ornate bracket lamps was that of E.W.Grimes & Co Ltd, a popular draper's shop. On the immediate right the five hanging lamps denote Halfords Cycle Co Ltd. Prior to 1906 a large ornate iron lamp standard stood in place of the statue. *FWS 744*

The Spot. A group of Edwardian children gathered around the rear of Queen Victoria's statue in 1908. Note the young butcher's boy with his bloodstained apron and the young boy with handcart. The narrow gabled front of the popular Cheshire Cheese public house is on the right.

The Morledge. This well animated original Scarratt photograph of 1908 was taken from the steps of the old Canal Tavern on Cockpit Hill. In the centre left was provision dealer Horace Leonard Rawson's well-known Morledge Banana Warehouse. A.E.Goddard boot factors on the right eventually transferred into the Market Hall. The Shot Tower dominates in the background. This and most of the buildings in view were demolished as part of Derby's modernisation programme, making way for the eventual Bus Station, Open Market, Council House and eventually the Eagle Centre.

The Rowditch. A classic well animated *c.*1908 photograph of the junction of Uttoxeter Old and New Roads ('The Rowditch') The driver of Derby Corporation electric tram car number 19 manages a smile for the camera as he prepares to pass the pony and trap parked outside the Rowditch Inn public house on the immediate left. This view would have been taken not long after the tram route was opened on 28 November 1907. Next door was George Gadsby's cycle dealer's shop; just round the corner is the entrance to the Rowditch Recreation Ground on Uttoxeter Old Road, purchased by the Corporation at a cost of £5,500. *FWS 207*

The Shot Tower, *c.*1908. One of Derby's best known landmarks was built in 1809 by Joseph Gascoyne for local lead merchants Messrs Cox and Poyser. They produced lead shot for guns by pouring molten lead from the top of the tower (over 180ft high) through sieves, whereafter small drops of solidified lead would be formed just before they landed in a water reservoir at the bottom. The tower was demolished by H.Lister & Son from Sheffield in 1932 to make way for the present Corporation Street. The Shot Tower corn store's of J.G.Fox were at the left of the tower base. *FWS 186*

Training College. Situated on Uttoxeter New Road, the former Lichfield and Southwell Diocesan College 'For Training School Mistresses' (inscription over the door in stone) opened in 1851. The founder was the Rt Revd John Lonsdale (Bishop of Lichfield) and the college was designed in red brick by Henry Isaac Stevens. The lady to the left of the entrance in this *c.*1914 scene is Scarratt's wife Mary. *FWS 921*

Victoria Street. A *c.*1912 view looking down Victoria Street towards Albert Street and the beginning of St Peter's Street. The newly-elected Town Council, under the 1835 Municipal Act, culverted Markeaton Brook between St Peter's and St James's Bridge and laid over it a new street named after the new queen in the first year of her reign. Cash & Co's famous large store stands on the corner of Green Lane. The Royal Hotel and Athenaeum spans the left-hand side. *FWS 599*

The Wardwick and Strand. Classic Scarratt photography in this 1907-08 view of The Wardwick. Open-top electric tram car number 6 is on its way to Uttoxeter Road. The young GPO boy on the right poses for FWS in the shadow of the wooden ladder. Culverting of the brook between St James's and Sadler Gate bridges started in 1863 and a new street was built over it, The Strand with its graceful curve following the brook course and officially opened in 1881. The Mechanics Institute building on the right adjacent to tram was rebuilt in 1881 in the Italian style by Arthur Coke Hill and G.H.Sheffield. The Derby Working Men's Association organised concerts here. Prior to rebuilding eminent people such as William Makepeace Thackery, Charles Dickens, and Franz Liszt performed here. Dominating the corner are the premises of Edgar Horn & Co, piano and organ merchants of some repute. This photograph was published in the *Derby Evening Telegraph.* *FWS 186*

The Wardwick. The policeman with white coat and gloves standing in his wooden platform carries out his point duties *c.*1930-31 at the intersection between The Wardwick and The Strand. The young lady pushes her low-lying pram across the cobbles towards the Post Office. This was published in the *Derby Evening Telegraph. FWS 1411*

The Free Library. The Free Library and Museum is pictured here in 1914, prior to its extension in 1915. It was originally built by R.Knil Freeman in 1879 of red brick in the domestic Flemish gothic style with a Franco-Flemish central tower. It was the gift of the late M.T.Bass. In 1911 there were 24,840 volumes in the Lending Library and 15,301 in the Reference Library. The curious gabled house of Dr Fox at the left (out of view) was demolished in 1914 to make way for the extension. *FWS 895*

The Wardwick. Early single-decker Trent Bus registration number CH 8255 ploughs through The Wardwick flood water of May 1932, passing the Mechanics Institute. On the right at number 6 stand the premises of Ernest Club & Co boot manufacturers. Behind the stranded car the provisions shop of Melias Ltd was on the left next to Alton & Co Ltd wine merchants. *FWS 1586*

St Werburgh's Church, *c.*1909. Situated in Friar Gate with a position at the junction of six main thoroughfares the church of St Werburgh's has almost certainly existed since AD700. The present tower dates from 1699 – the medieval fabric collapsed in November 1698 after yet another Derby flood – and the rest was built to its present style (late decorated) in 1893-94, from designs by Sir A.W.Bloomfield. The tower contains a clock and eight bells. The register dates from 1588 and contains the record of the marriage of Dr Samuel Johnson in 1735. *FWS 284*

St Werburgh's Church interior. Taken in *c*.1914-15, this photograph shows the intricate chancel screen and choir stalls which were erected in 1898 by W.Ralph Smith Esq. The magnificent wrought-iron pulpit on the left was by Sir Arthur Bloomfield and was presented by Mr Grimwood Taylor. There were originally 900 seatings. The church was closed to worship in the 1980s and later became a shopping gallery with a tea room and restaurant, although trade was never buoyant and at the time of writing there are apparently plans to hand the building back to a church group. *FWS 832*

Derby. A five panel multi-view showing Derbyshire Royal Infirmary, Littleover Hollow, Duffield Road, the Arboretum entrance and The Wardwick. It was produced *c*.1910. *FWS 380*

Derby. A vertical three-panel multi-view featuring the River Derwent, Cathedral interior and St Peter's Street (showing the large Midland Drapery store complete with its famous magnet sign). The card was produced in *c.*1928 from previous single-issue postcards. *FWS 1389*

Derby. A 1914 production five-panel multi-view showing The Spot, Normanton Recreation Ground, the Guildhall, the Arboretum and Littleover Hollow. Scarratt was famed for these popular five-in-one multi-views with a palette centre border. *FWS 824*

Derby. An extremely scarce *c.*1908 Scarratt three-panel multi-view. This is the only one of this design (centre circular panel) so far found. The top view shows open-top electric tram car number 4 passing through Friar Gate towards the town centre. The elegant residences on the right usually housed doctors, surgeons and other worthies. The other views – Green Lane and Mile Ash Lane – were issued as separate views. *FWS 260*

Ashbourne Road. In this *c.*1912 view looking towards what is now Markeaton Park, the handcart, horse and cart and open-top tram compete for space. The old Congregational church on the right had seating for 500. It was severely damaged by fire in 1994. The shop on the immediate left is Miss Hall's confectionery shop. The ray of sunshine on the left pavement near the hand cart is emanating from Fowler Street with Mrs Martha E.Parker's tripe shop on the corner. *FWS 636*

St John's Church. Situated in Bridge Street, this church was erected in 1828 at a cost of £7,500. It was an elegant gothic structure in the later English style with heavily ornamented octagonal turrets with projected castellated tops and nine long windows on each side. This was a coloured view of the Anglican church and one of the earliest known Scarratt publications, *c.*1906. It was built by Messrs Bridgart to the designs of Francis Goodwin. It was the first church to be consecrated since the Reformation. Much cast-iron fittings, tracery and decoration was incorporated from the Derby founders of Messrs Weatherhead, Glover & Co of Duke Street. The cupolas were removed from each tower before 1900. The building to the left with pinnacles in the roof is that of an old school built *c.*1840. The smoking chimney (left) belongs to the Friar Gate Laundry. Horse-drawn carts would normally park along side the railings. *FWS 79*

Burton Road. This *c.*1910 scene shows Derby Corporation tram car number 121 approaching the crest of the hill towards the old tram terminus close to Vicarage Road (right). The fine Edwardian turreted house on the right stands today. The tram route opened in 1904 and closed in 1932. *FWS 325*

Burton Road. This *c.*1911-12 view looks towards Littleover and shows an open-top tram approximately level with Abbey Street on the top right. The fine ornate houses with gothic style gables on the right look good today. The distant Mount Carmel tower is that of the old Mason's paint works chimney, designed by G.Thompson in 1869 and is now the site of a garage. This photograph was also issued as number 1058. *FWS 411*

Burton Road. This early view of *c*.1910 shows electric tram car number 21 having passed Mount Carmel steps on the right on its way to the Market Place. Shops on the corner of Abbey Street are just visible on the left. The spire of Christ Church on Normanton Road can be seen in the distant left. *FWS 338*

Chester Green. Sturdy wooden frameworks for the children's swings were positioned on either side of the pavilion on Little Chester Recreation Ground, off Mansfield Road. In this mid 1920s view the little boy is holding his dog next to the swings. This photograph was published in the *Derby Evening Telegraph*. *FWS 1235*

St Paul's Church, *c.* 1927. Situated on Mansfield Road overlooking Chester Green, this church was consecrated in 1850 by the Lord Bishop of Lichfield. One of the chief contributors to the building fund was the father of Colonel Pountain. It is a cruciform building of stone in the decorated style, with a single bell tower and surmounted by a spirelet at one corner. *FWS 1319*

Duffield Road. At the intersection of Kedleston and Duffield Roads stood the famous Derby landmark 'The Five Lamps'. The iron work was cast by Messrs Weatherhead, Glover & Co in 1839 and the lamps originally stood on the Cornmarket at St Peter's Bridge near the Royal Hotel. To improve traffic flow they were resited here in *c.* 1905. In this *c.* 1914 picture the central globe of the magnificent quintuple is an inferior replacement to the original. A similar quintuple lamp standard also existed at 'The Five Lamps' at the bottom of Normanton Road. Electric tram car number 44 is on its way up Kedleston Road. Note the man cleaning out the tram tracks near the Five Lamps. *FWS 892*

Duffield Road. At one time this was the main road north out of Derby. The east side bordered the park of St Helen's House (that of Darley Hall) and the estate was built over from 1891. The prestigious houses on the east side were built for successful local businessmen. In this *c.*1914 scene it is not clear why the man and his delivery bike are facing the wrong direction up Duffield Road. The heavy iron posts and chain links date back to 1881. The retaining stone work was renovated in 1989. *FWS 893*

Duffield Road. This *c.*1912 winter scene looking towards Duffield just above Highfield Road (left) shows the end of the iron posts and chains as the road and pavement levels become equal. The large tree on the left is much larger and now next to a modern bungalow. The large house hidden by the trees is situated just below Burleigh Drive and is now the Mulberry Day Nursery. The gate post immediate right leads to a splendid turreted house number 174 called 'Haye Leigh'. *FWS 689*

This *c.*1908 rural view of Mile Ash Lane shows an open-top motor vehicle coming from Darley Abbey, well before the houses and walls of the present day were built. The cast-iron sign today on the side of the cottages lower down and out of view, wrongly refers to 'Miles Ash'. *FWS 243*

Friar Gate, *c.*1908. Open-top electric tram car number 2 is about to pass under the famous ornate iron bridge carrying the Great Northern Railway over the main Derby-Ashbourne road. The bridge was made by the famous firm of Andrew Handyside & Co of Derby during 1876-78. Two GNR servants are just visible carrying out maintenance work on the semaphore signal to the right above the wooden carriages of the milk van on the bridge. The handcart and basket on the left belong to the Derby Coal Co which operated from the curved stone fronted building adjoining the bridge (this is now a sandwich shop). Friar Gate Station, which was built partly on the site of the former White Horse Inn, opened in 1878 and closed in 1964. *FWS 204*

Halfpenny Lane. Five fine young Derby lads enjoy time out from school down by the small brook *c*.1913. The view of the brook has long since gone in this quaint little lane situated near Sherwin Street and Newton's Walk and, like Penny Long Lane, emerging into Broadway.
FWS 762

Friar Gate. A busy scene *c.*1912 looking towards the town centre from the corner of Stafford Street. The tramways are alive with horse-drawn vehicles and dogs. Derby's first Dissenting Chapel, the Unitarian, can be seen behind the tram wire pole on the right. It was erected in 1698 as a Presbyterian Chapel and in 1782 it was sold to the Unitarians, the Strutt family paying the bill. The large house on the corner of Stafford Street was called the County Club (formerly the Portland Temperance Club) which, along with the chapel, have since been demolished and replaced by an ugly office block. The London plane trees were planted in 1869 from money raised from subscriptions. In the distant left is the quadruple gables of F.P.Copestake & Sons' grocery emporium. The house on the immediate left was that of Alderman Gilbert Chesshyre and known as the Queen Anne House, built in 1708 and demolished in 1938 as part of the Ford Street widening scheme. *FWS 635*

Kedleston Road. A superb 1910 close up of electric tram balcony car number 30 as it sedately glides past the horse-drawn cab. The heavily ivy-clad irregular-shaped eighteenth-century house on the right with the neat lace curtains is The Elms. At this time it was a preparatory branch of Derby School (there is a sign on the railings). It was later to house a dentistry practice and although still there today, the ornate upper brickwork has gone and it is in dire need of expert renovation. Two of the ornate famous Five Lamps are visible top right. *FWS 331*

Kedleston Road. This was an early coloured Scarratt publication of 1905-06 showing St Aiden's Church on the corner of Cedar Street. This church was known as the 'Iron Church' due to its corrugated iron fabric, and was classed as a mission hall. Scarratt's father, Thomas, planted the two silver birch trees on the corner of this view. The tram car has just passed Longford Street. *FWS 96*

Kedleston Road. A busy *c.*1911 scene looking towards town with lots of animation, push chairs, prams, hand carts, cycles etc. On the left at the corner of Bromley Street stands the premises of Turner, Calvert & Daykin who were chemists and a local sub-Post Office (letter box to right of shop). A chemist's shop has remained here for many years. The pony and cart appears to be on a collision course with the tram. *FWS 425*

Kedleston Road. This *c*.1908 photograph was taken from Redshaw Street (on the left) looking up Kedleston Road towards Markeaton. Open-top electric tram car number 11 is passing the elegant three-storey houses between Statham Street and Wheeldon Avenue, on the right. Scarratt's son Alec stands by the large tree on the corner of Statham Street. *FWS 206*

Kedleston Road. This *c*.1913 view taken just above Bromley Street show the pony and trap passing the railings of Kedleston Road Council School. The distant tram on the right has just passed Cedar Street. *FWS 746*

Kedleston Road Council Schools. This *c.*1912 view shows the girls' school with the word 'Girls' over both left and right entrances. This public elementary school on Kedleston Road was originally erected to accommodate 356 boys, 356 girls and 320 infants. Arthur Hayman (master), Miss E.Bennett (girls' mistress) and Miss F.Redfearn (infants' mistress) were formerly in charge. The railings disappeared during World War Two as part of the war effort. The adjacent Parkfield Cedars School for Girls, a grammar school, opened in the old house in 1918. *FWS 675*

Cowley Street. This was an early coloured *c.*1907 scene looking up Cowley Street towards Kedleston Road and is part of Scarratt's early FWS 'Abbey' series. The Victoria Hotel public house, built by Offilers Brewery, stands on the corner of Watson Street in the old West End of Derby. The railings on the right were part of Markeaton Recreation Ground, a nine-acre site presented to the town by F.N.Mundy Esq of Markeaton in 1895. *FWS 133*

The West End. This superb photograph is probably Scarratt's most famous and was taken *c.*1907 and issued as part of his FWS 'Abbey' series and also published in the *Derby Evening Telegraph* several times over the years. The West End, situated north of Ashbourne Road and Friar Gate, was once classed as one of Derby's poorest areas, producing many colourful characters and much folklore. Much 18th-century industry (tape mills etc) existed here. This scene shows people hurrying to work along Brook Walk. The iron lattice work bridge carried a footpath from Searle Street and was removed in 1978. The Brookside and Brook Street area included the Derby Smallware Co (since 1880) which made boot loops, W.Dyer, a silk throwster and manufacturer originally of Canal Street (1871) and Abell's Foundry which produced a range of castings. Prior to 1903, Scarratt worked for Wilkins & Ellis, who had a paper staining works opposite Abell's factory. The ornate castellations of St John's Church in nearby Bridge Street are in the background. *FWS 132*

London Road. Many horse-drawn and early motor vehicles make their way along London Road in this *c.*1910 view looking towards The Spot. The open-top tram car has just passed the old Congregational Chapel which later became the Coliseum cinema. On the right corner of Traffic Street stands the Telegraph Inn (now Strutts public house). The Victoria Laundry which stands on the immediate right is today the gentlemen's hairdressing salon of Joe Gallagher. The narrow Bradshaw Street is on the left next to the building advertising Raleigh Cycles. The plane trees were instituted by Jon Davis and planted in 1869. *FWS 328*

London Road. This *c.*1914 view looking towards the town centre shows the Crompton & Evans Bank building of 1912 on the corner of Midland Road, built on the site of J.Ravensdale's butcher's shop. On the opposite corner is the fine 1853 building of the Crown and Cushion public house run by Arthur Felix. On the left is the large ornate gabled building starting on the corner with Regent Street and housing several banking chambers associated with the mining industry. Later it became a Salvation Army hostel and is presently called Magee Court. The tower of Holy Trinity is in the distant right. *FWS 760*

London Road. This *c.*1913 view is looking from Midland Road towards Crewton and Alvaston. On the right is the Midland Garage of Charles Henry Guest. The open-top tram is level with Oxford Street on the right and is about to pass St Andrew's Church on the left. The smart policeman is on point duty at the junction with Midland Road. This was previously issued as postcard number 708. *FWS 1061*

LMS Railway Cenotaph. The Cenotaph in this *c*.1927 view is situated on Midland Road (former Station Street) close to the Midland Hotel, to commemorate railway staff who died in World War One. The Midland Hotel building was by Francis Thompson, the first Midland Railway architect, and was the first railway hotel in the country. *FWS 1335*

Derbyshire Royal Infirmary. This is one of the few unnumbered postcards taken by Scarratt in 1908-09, showing the main drive to the Infirmary, which was given the 'Royal' title by Queen Victoria at its reopening when she laid the foundation stone in 1891.

Florence Nightingale monument. Florence Nightingale lived at Lea Hurst near Matlock and became known as the 'Lady of the Lamp' during the Crimean War. The monument was unveiled by the Duke of Devonshire in 1924, and is situated outside the Derbyshire Royal Infirmary, where Florence Nightingale had taught. The sculptress was H.S.H.Princess Feodora v Hohemlohe Langenburg (Countess Gleachen 1861-1922). To the right is the ivy-clad nurses home built in 1893. This card is also unnumbered.

Midland Station. The ornate iron tram wire and lamp structure stands on the left outside the York Commercial Hotel run by Thomas Charles Sanders in this *c.*1912 view. The fine station façade designed by Francis Thompson has now disappeared, being replaced by an inferior modern design in 1985. *FWS 586*

Traffic Street. In this late 1930s scene, taken from where Bradshaw Street meets London Road, Scarratt has captured the neat and recently widened Traffic Street running down to Siddals Road, to the Ice Factory island. The street was officially opened by the Lord Mayor of London. The Coliseum cinema with its Corinthian columns was originally built by Derby architect Henry I. Stevens in 1843 as the Congregational Chapel. It was converted by T.H.Thorpe and opened as a cinema in 1934. To the right of the entrance, adjacent to the parked cars, a sign displays 'Patrons free car-park' (although it looks to hold a maximum of six vehicles only). This photographic postcard was posted in 1938, and the advertising hoardings show that *Paradise Isle* and *Old Mother Riley* were showing at that time. The building was demolished as part of a further rewidening scheme for Traffic Street in 1962. On the bottom right, on the corner of Copeland Street, stood the former Primative Methodist Chapel, and at the top right the Derby Town Mission. *FWS 1804*

St Andrew's interior. The church was peculiarly rich in stained-glass. The fine ornate oak screen by the south porch was erected in 1885 at a cost of £170. Originally there were 900 sittings. The pillars were alternately round and octagonal as seen in this view *c.*1915. *FWS 978*

St Andrew's Church, seen here in 1910, was essentially a 'railway church'. The Midland Railway Co contributed generously to the building fund to ensure that its growing army of employees were adequately ministered. The corner stone was laid in 1864 by the Duke of Devonshire and was completed 1866-67 to designs by Sir Gilbert Scott RA, of St Pancras Station fame. Its spire, some 200ft high, was a landmark as far away as Alvaston, Normanton, Chaddesden, Spondon and even Quarndon. It was demolished in 1970 and the site is now occupied by the Department of Social Security. *FWS 334*

Old Normanton: Two views of St Giles's Church on Village Street. Owing to its limited size the former church with Norman and fourteenth-century fabric was demolished on 27 May 1861. The new building consisted of chancel, nave, south aisle, tower and weather cock crowned spire dedicated to St Giles and was opened in 1862. The exterior material was freestone, hammer dressed. It was extended in 1893 and again in 1902-03 when a new nave and chancel were added. The church had close associations with the Sherwood Foresters during World War One and contains many memorials to the men who died. *FWS 428 & FWS 507*

Normanton Recreation Ground. Known by many Derbeians as 'Normo Rec', this was officially opened by the Duke of Devonshire on 4 September 1909. This scene from 1911 shows the girls' swings and play area. Boys were not officially allowed here as they had their own separate playground. However, one small boy in shorts (right) appears to have challenged the system. This photograph also appeared in the *Derby Evening Telegraph*. *FWS 467*

Normanton Recreation Ground. This is a closer view than the previous and shows the sturdiness of the swings. Over 40 young girls appear in this 1911 scene. This photographic postcard was posted on 30 August 1911 and the message reads: "Dear Daddy, Thank you for PC. This is where I see-saw. I do so like it. With lots of love, Mary." The swings, see-saws and slides gradually deteriorated and were eventually replaced by an open play area containing modern equipment. *FWS 466*

Normanton Recreation Ground. A nice touch as the gentleman sitting on the park bench lifts his straw boater to the ladies out for a leisurely Sunday stroll during the summer of *c.*1911. The pavilion is in the background. Mary Scarratt and daughter are believed to be on the right. This photograph appeared in the *Derby Evening Telegraph. FWS 468*

Normanton Recreation Ground. On a late summer's day afternoon *c.*1910 this proved to be a popular place for many local children. The double gabled building complete with clock tower on the left, fronts the pavilion style construction. Between the gables is the stone plaque inscribed: 'County Borough of Derby. Normanton Recreation Grounds, opened by the Duke of Devonshire, 4 September 1909. Cornelius Boam Chairman, W.Blews Robotham Mayor.' The structure has now almost been rebuilt but the plaque remains. New bay windows have been fitted together with a TV aerial. *FWS 360*

Dairyhouse Road. In this *c.*1912 view Scarratt has captured the serenity of the day as the electric tram car glides its way past Cambridge Street and the Cambridge Hotel (left). On the opposite corner of Cambridge Street is Harry Lewis's butcher's shop. A light sprinkling of snow is apparent on the pavement alongside the railings outside of the United Methodist Chapel (right). *FWS 601*

Rose Hill Street. This scarce *c.*1912 photograph of Rose Hill Street was taken from the junction of Molineux Street and Grange Street (at the end of Malcolm Street) looking towards Normanton Road. The three white-smocked children are playing outside the elegant ivy-clad residences of Kenmore Villas and Rose Hill Terrace with their ornate wrought-iron railings. In the distant right are the railings and lodge entrance house to the famous Arboretum. Rose Hill Street was *the* place to live and deserves a better reputation today. *FWS 706*

St Joseph's Church, *c.*1911. Situated on Gordon Road is St Joseph's Roman Catholic Church originally built in 1879 as a school chapel and rebuilt in 1897 at a cost of £4,000. It was an edifice of brick with stone dressings in the gothic style and was Derby's second Catholic church after the Reformation. Today the church has changed dedications to the Polish St Maksymilian Kolbe. The presbytery is the building on the left. *FWS 409*

Christ Church, *c.*1912. This church was built on the west side of Normanton Road and erected in 1839-40. The spire is 350ft above sea level. The structure is in the Early English style. The tower buttresses are ornamented, the pinnacles crocketed and the light flying buttresses support the huge spire in its rise from the tower. The Unity Hall building was to the right and has now been demolished. The church is no longer dedicated as such and is now the Serbian Orthodox Church of the Holy Apostles Peter and Paul. *FWS 469*

The Arboretum: Joseph Strutt purchased land to the rear of the workhouse on Osmaston Road and engaged one of the foremost landscape artists in the country, Mr Loudon, to design the layout of the country's first public park. He gave his name to nearby Loudon Street. The Arboretum was opened on 16 September 1840, not long after the introduction of the Victorian 'Penny Black' postage stamp. In this *c.*1912 picture, Scarratt's daughter Winnie poses for her father in front of the famous iron Arboretum fountain built by Weatherhead & Glover, a firm eventually taken over by A.Handyside & Co of Duke Street. This photograph appeared in the *Derby Evening Telegraph. FWS 576*

A later view of the Arboretum Fountain, probably *c.*1912 showing that the fountain with its neat rockery garden was a popular meeting place for young and old alike. This photograph was obviously taken on a Sunday with the locals dressed in their finery. The distinguished gentleman with white beard obliges for the camera, whilst the ladies exchange gossip. It is believed that several members of the Scarratt family are in this picture, wife and daughter right, son left. The man with the white beard also appears in a Donkey Lane, Littleover, view (number 131) and is possibly Scarratt's father-in-law. *FWS 709*

The Arboretum. Scarratt's daughter Winnie again composing herself in this *c.*1912 scene at the entrance to the Arboretum with the ivy-clad arcade in the background. Note the extremely neat lawn edging. *FWS 578*

Arboretum Aviary. Several straw-hatted locals peer into the Aviary *c.*1912, probably looking at its famous inhabitant. 'Arboretum Polly', a very popular parrot, dwelt here for nearly 40 years and is now preserved in Derby Museum after skilled work by a taxidermist in 1919. *FWS 577*

The Arboretum Boar. The Florentine Boar was donated to the park by its founder Joseph Strutt. It was made of Italian marble designed by John Coffee. Over 100 years many Derby children were photographed next to it. It is now missing, allegedly removed following damage during World War Two. Note the strings of lights above each side of the footpath in this 1935 view. *FWS 1678*

The Arboretum Fountain. Yet another view of the ornate fountain, this time frozen over during the winter of 1913. This postcard publication was posted on 18 January 1914 and the message reads 'All well at Derby, we have been to church this morning. Revd. P preached. Here is the Arboretum.' *FWS 867*

The Arboretum. Showing the aviary, fountain and entrance, probably produced c.1912. Scarratt's wife Mary is on the park bench in the centre view. *FWS 666*

Nottingham Road. Electric tram car number 41 glides down 'Cemetery Hill' on a single-track from Chaddesden passing the horse-drawn cab parked outside Joseph Mason & Co Ltd's varnish and paint works on Nottingham Road *c.*1910. The Chaddesden Lace Works Institute was next door to the works. In the distance behind the tram, the tower of the New Cemetery entrance arch is just visible. This photograph appeared in the *Derby Evening Telegraph. FWS 363*

Osmaston Hall. This magnificent hall, seen here in *c.*1910, was originally built in 1696 and was once situated in the Wilmot family estate of 3,700 acres within Osmaston-by-Derby, close to the present Ascot Drive industrial estate on the east side of Osmaston Road. The Midland Railway bought the hall and estate in 1888 from Sir Rodney Robert Wilmot for £90,000 for use as offices, but later sold it to Derby County Borough. It was demolished in 1938. *FWS 358*

Osmaston Church. This is a *c.*1910 view of St James's Church which was situated close to Osmaston Hall. C.J.Payne, in his 1893 book, *Derby Churches Old and New* referred to it as 'that queer little church'. He also stated: 'As the Midland Railway Company require the ground it appears probable that the present church will suffer removal'. It was indeed subsequently demolished and the burial ground de-consecrated. Many monuments to the Wilmots of Chaddesden existed. The dedication of this church was once referred to as being All Saints'. *FWS 359*

Osmaston Road. This *c.*1910 scene is looking north towards the town centre, and shows electric open-top tram car number 24 travelling towards the Baptist Chapel on the corner of Charnwood Street. This was demolished and replaced with a modern edifice in 1970. Grove Street is on the left and most of the elegant houses on the right, some dating from the 1820s, have had to make way for various extensions to the Derbyshire Royal Infirmary. *FWS 362*

Rolls-Royce. Both views, *c.*1913, were commissioned for sale as postcards by Beatrice A.Sidley at her St Dunstan's Post Office at 468 Osmaston Road. The works were opened on 9 July 1908 on an 11-acre site and constructed by Handyside & Co. Henry Royce soon had in excess of 400 skilled workers and brought great fame to the town of Derby and, over the years, jobs for thousands of local people, rivalling the railways for employment. Initially the Derby works manufactured motor cars and engines such as the world-famous Silver Ghost, but between the wars, aero engines became the prime product. The first Rolls-Royce aero engine was the Eagle, which was on test in 1915, and by the end of World War One more than 4,000 Eagle and 2,000 Falcon engines were produced. *FWS 820 & FWS 821*

Osmaston Road. This *c.*1912 view looks from the town down Osmaston Road. The elegant ivy-clad house with Venetian blinds stood on the corner of Bloomfield Street, now Bloomfield Court. The tram car is approaching the corner of Reginald Street. This junction is now served by traffic lights and that section of the road is now a short dual carriageway running down to Ivy Square. *FWS 707*

St Luke's Church. Situated in the neglected district of 'California' and dedicated to St Luke the beloved physician, this church was consecrated in 1871 to provide a ministry for the growing population of the area. The architect was F.J.Robinson of Derby. It has ten stained-glass lancet windows in the chancel with cuspings in the heads. The nave is lit by five plate tracery windows in the south. The pulpit as seen in this *c.*1914 view was made of marble, in the form of an ambo with steps on either side, and was the gift of Miss Lonsdale. *FWS 833*

Further into the Suburbs

Allestree. This *c.*1907 illustration, originally coloured, shows the small brick building of Mr Chas Herbert Corner's blacksmith shop. Edwardian children used to pay frequent visits to their local smithy. A former famous Allestree landmark, a huge whalebone, is just out of camera shot in the rear garden. The former Allestree Park gates and ivy-clad South Lodge to Allestree Hall are in the centre (Evans Avenue starts here now). All is very different now, this being the busy A6 main road to Matlock and Manchester. The corner house and adjoining buildings still stand and from left to right are a pet food shop, hair salon and private house on the corner of Park Lane. *FWS 147*

Allestree Church. A mid-afternoon view of St Edmund's taken *c.*1908. The church was rebuilt and enlarged by the late Sir T.W.Evans in 1866-67 in the Early English style at a cost of £6,000. The chancel contained many monuments to the Mundy Family and had close ties with Lionel Guy Gisbourne of Allestree Hall, who in 1913 gave a gift of land for an extension to the churchyard. *FWS 232*

Alvaston. What a contrast in this *c.*1925 scene of a young girl in a simple white frock trying her luck with fishing net, while her heavily robed family watching from the nearby seat. Alvaston Lake was constructed in 1923 with five acres of water and was initially stocked with all kinds of fish. The site was part of the London Road Recreation Ground of some 25 acres, created for Derby Corporation by Barrons in 1913. *FWS 1258*

This is an early 1930s view looking down London Road (at the end of Shardlow Road) to its junction with Alvaston Street on the right (now Raynesway). This was the Alvaston tram terminus. The London Road tram route (Harrington Arms-Alvaston) opened on 27 July 1904 and closed on 22 July 1932. The tram has just passed the chimney belonging to the Alvaston steam laundry. 'Ye Olde Sweet Shoppe' of William Fleming is on the left and with its many enamelled advertising signs would be an antique collector's dream today. At one time there was a little 'jitty' to the side of Fleming's which led to a small billiard hall. *FWS 1480*

Alvaston. A fine close up of electric tram car number 32 passing the Carnegie Library on London Road at the entrance to Alvaston Lake and Recreation Ground c.1931. The Carnegie Library was a fine looking building situated in the area of Crewton and was named after Andrew Carnegie, the world famous philanthropist of Carnegie Hall (New York) fame. He decided that the working class needed to read and write as he thought they were being kept in ignorance and therefore unable to improve their lot. The building and furniture were completed in May 1916 and initially only the reading room was opened. It was designed by Arthur Eaton. This Carnegie Library closed in 1971 and was demolished in 1980. What was originally a Carnegie Library in Pear Tree is still in use, now part of the Derbyshire County Library Service. *FWS 1482*

Alvaston. An extremely scarce c.1931 photograph of London Road looking towards the Alvaston Hotel (now the Roundhouse) taken from the Alvaston tram terminus. The original Harrington Arms Hotel advertising Allsopp's Burton Ales is on the left, next to the Derby Co-operative Society Ltd building, the Harrington Arms building was demolished in 1966. The lone cyclist has just passed the well known Peach's pork pie shop on the right. The railings on the right housed the Alvaston steam laundry with its gravel drive with neat lawns and borders either side. Eden Street ran to the right of Peach's pork pie shop and a small yard was home to a local blacksmith. Locals remember long wartime ration queues stretching from the Co-op down the road and into the yard of the Harrington Arms. *FWS 1483*

Alvaston. An unusually quiet early 1930s scene with children coming home from school along Shardlow Road from the direction of Derby. Compare this with the dense traffic along the A6 today. The 'monkey' tree on the right is now much bigger. The large white house in the distant left with the 'B.O.P.' – *Boy's Own Paper* – advertisement on the side was Merry's newsagent's shop. The large adjacent house (left) was Mr Wain's private school, which has since been demolished and the Stanhope Lodge public house built in its place. To the right of the three boys, Petersham Drive was built. The three gabled houses on the right exist today. *FWS 1486*

Alvaston. The old house on the right has long since gone, but the council houses (as built) on the left survived road widening and the creation of Raynesway to replace the former Alvaston Street. The Raynesway dual carriageway appeared in the early 1930s – Beech Avenue is now near here. Number 144 is the nearest of the stucco faced council houses in this early 1930s scene. *FWS 1486*

Alvaston. Two gentleman take time out for a chat and a rest on The Green, now the Blue Peter island. The first building on the left is the former parochial church hall for Boulton Church, called the Star Rooms Place of Worship, which is now utilised as Murfin's flower and greengrocery shop, the houses to the right being demolished and replaced by thriving shops. This view is looking towards Raynesway and London Road *c.*1931. *FWS 1487*

Borrowash. Finely dressed young ladies cycle down Victoria Avenue smiling at FWS in this *c.*1907 picture (issued as a brown colour print) looking towards Ockbrook. FWS's sister is thought to be on the left and his wife centre. *FWS 128*

Borrowash. This was an early coloured illustration of the old Wilmot Arms public house on the right-hand side of Derby Road, looking towards Borrowash village centre *c*.1907. The old Forresters Arms public house is just visible in the distance. *FWS 138*

Borrowash. This *c*.1909 view (unnumbered) shows a steam train in the distance with the stationmaster on the right. The ornate gabled building on the left-hand platform carried many advertisements. This station (resited west of the Station Road bridge instead of east as earlier) was opened on 1 May 1871. It closed in 1966 but some of the station buildings survived until being demolished in 1984.

Borrowash. This is one of Scarratt's classic real photographic types showing his brother Albert cycling up Nottingham Road. Albert is also managing to push Scarratt's own bicycle. The tradesman in the white coat is painting the fine gabled building on the right of this *c.*1914 scene. Behind the walled hedge lay the tennis court which is there today. *FWS 851*

Borrowash. This *c.*1914 view is looking up Gordon Road, with the fine houses with their ornamental iron gates and railings on the left. Station Road is at the top right. *FWS 852*

Borrowash. This mid-1930s view shows the many large greenhouses and small water tower belonging to the well known nurseries of William Barron & Son. This local firm was famed for its garden landscaping and worked on the London Road Recreation Ground. The intricate cross-shaped fish pond and many fine garden ornaments are featured. *FWS 1735*

Breadsall. Brookside is situated off Rectory Lane in Breadsall and often referred to by knowledgeable locals as Frog Lane due to nearby large residence formerly named Frog Hall. The young farmer's boy is facing the Boosemoor Brook running to the left of the picture; his cows are heading home to Clewes Farm through the wall on the right. The large house shown in this early 1920s scene is called Willow Springs. *FWS 1150*

Breadsall. These two views show the burnt-out shell of Breadsall's All Saints' Church, the fire on 4 June 1914 allegedly started by Suffragettes. The blaze destroyed beautiful wooden carvings, an ornate rude screen and a double reading desk containing invaluable works of the Reformation period. The interior of the church was restored in 1914-16 at a cost of £11,000, reopening on 14 April 1916. Much of the restoration work was carried by a Mr Caroe. The rector at the time was Revd John Ayton Whittaker. *FWS 944 & 945*

Breadsall. This 1914 view looking up Church Street towards All Saints' may have been taken shortly after the fire as at least three people are looking at something over the church wall, a theory apparently substantiated by Scarratt's sequential numbering and copyright note. However, damage is not easily apparent in this view. The white building on the left was the local Post Office of Frederick Thomas Endsor who was parish clerk as well as sub-Post Master. There is still a Post Office there today. The house on the right is Church House. *FWS 943*

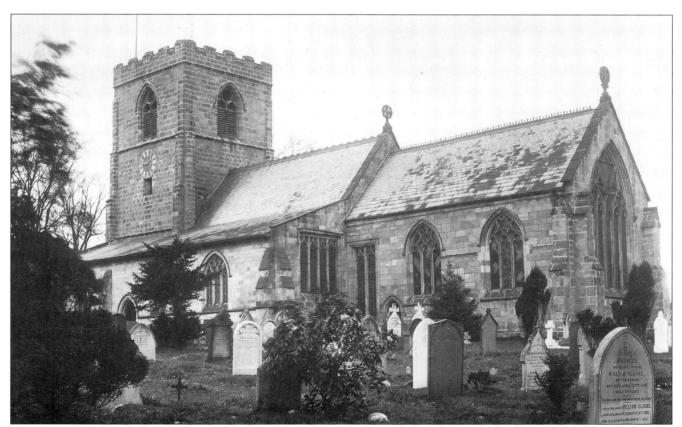

Chaddesden. This *c.*1908 view shows the stone church of St Mary at Chaddesden. It is of the gothic style consisting of chancel, nave of three bays, aisles and a perpendicular western tower with embattled parapet. The tower was restored and a new clock provided in 1903. Many memorials to the Wilmot family are contained here. *FWS 228*

Chaddesden. The cemetery on Chaddesden Hill covered an area of 43 acres, being opened in 1855 at a cost of £23,500 and containing two mortuary chapels. This was a coloured view entitled 'New Cemetery' and was taken in late 1908. *FWS 192*

Chellaston. This *c.*1906 view, published as a coloured postcard, is looking up the High Street towards St Peter's Church and was printed in Germany. Scarratt has written some important information on the back: 'Sent to Karl Liebhart on 9 December 1906, received 20 May 1907. 1,000 copies at 35s.' At this time Germany had the colour printing techniques that were not available in Britain, even if it did take the Germans six months to print and deliver the job. *FWS 100*

Chellaston. A local resident with her child and dog smiles for FWS's camera outside John Rayne's shop in the High Street during 1932. The little girl in the white dress is standing in the doorway of Forman's shop. The three houses on the top right were known as the 'steps houses' as each had a number of stone steps. They were demolished in the 1960s to make way for flats. The turning into Lime Avenue is on the right opposite the girl on the bicycle and was known locally as Charlie's Yard. *FWS 1549*

Chellaston. Scarratt took this view in 1932 from St Peter's Church tower looking down the High Street towards Station Road. The New Inn Pin public house (now the Corner Pin) is just visible at the bottom. The Wesleyan Chapel dating from 1875 is in the middle right. The six bay-fronted houses with their neatly laid out gardens have been *in situ* for a only short while. The roof and chimney in the immediate left foreground was known as the 'Yews'. The steps houses are on the left adjacent to the telegraph pole. *FWS 1548*

Chellaston. This view taken in 1914 is looking up Swarkestone Road with Scarratt's motor bike parked outside Mrs Jane Pym's shop and three-storey house on the left. To the rear of the fine gas lamp on the right stands J.William Bradley's New Inn public house selling Derby's famous Alton Ales. The pub is now renamed the Corner Pin. Just a short distance away lies Arthur Hodgkinson's Rose and Crown public house selling Marston's Ales. *FWS 908*

Chellaston. This is probably Scarratt's brother Albert with motor bike and sidecar travelling down the High Street towards the main Swarkestone Road. He also appears in the illustration at the top of this page, near the New Inn. Frederick Gilbert's large private residence The Lawn (now an hotel) is on the left. On both this and the preceding illustration Scarratt has recorded: 'Rotary 250 off, sent 9 April 1914, received 25 May 1914, sold out 1920.' This gives an insight into the scarcity of the cards. One wonders how many survived. *FWS 909*

Littleover. The two ladies with their prams are out for a summer stroll in this *c.*1910 scene. The view is taken at the entrance into Littleover from the junction with North Street looking up Burton Road. The small boy is inspecting the excavations on the left. The large houses standing in their own grounds on the right were converted into shops in the 1970s. *FWS 339*

Littleover. This wintery view is looking up Burton Road towards Derby in *c.*1914. The old village Post Office once famed for its rose garden, is on the right, a site now occupied by a petrol station. *FWS 863*

Littleover. This *c.*1913 scene shows the Scarratts out for a stroll down the quaint Donkey Lane (now North Street). Its name was derived from the donkeys kept in a nearby field. The rickety fencing, stile and gate have long gone. *FWS 805*

Littleover. This *c.*1932 view of Shepherd Street shows the half-timbered building of the White Swan public house which replaced an early eighteenth-century inn. Fairs and markets were once held in this area. The young man on his bicycle poses by the yard entrance. Scarratt's car is parked at the top near the old Co-op (later a library). *FWS 1542*

Littleover. In the distance Mrs Scarratt waits patiently by their car while Frank captures yet another scarce view of Derby's suburbs. This time three young boys are captured in Normanton Lane *c.*1932 alongside the fine bay-windowed brick houses to the right. *FWS 1543*

Littleover. This view of the Hollow in *c.*1909 is dominated by Littleover's famous sixteenth-century timber-framed cottage. It is Littleover's oldest building and was a former public house. At the turn of the century it was thatched. Originally the cottage was probably part of the Harpur estate with the old wattle and daub walls being replaced by brickwork. This charming relic has been much renovated over the years. Mr and Mrs Haynes and their dogs compose themselves outside the cottage for Scarratt's camera. This was previously issued as postcard number 370. *FWS 1055*

Littleover. This photographic postcard was posted in August 1920, but its low number suggests it was in the first batch to be published from 115 Normanton Road in *c.*1910. In this wintery scene a distinguished white-bearded old man steers his pony and trap up the Hollow, passing the three gentlemen in their heavy overcoats. *FWS 399*

Littleover. Well known Littleover inhabitant Mr Haynes stands smoking his pipe near Scarratt's motor bike whilst FWS's two brothers Albert (left) and Thomas cycle down the Hollow in *c*.1916. *FWS 1054*

Littleover. Many people along with Scarratt's two brothers can be seen riding or walking down the leafy Hollow towards the ancient stone troughs (left) *c*.1916. These are a reminder of the time when horses would drink the clear cool water during hot summer days. *FWS 1056*

Littleover. The Hollow was once the main road into Littleover from the south. In this *c.*1914 snow scene a small group of children with their toboggan make their way down the Hollow past the ancient cottage. *FWS 865*

Mackworth. A young lady, probably F.W.Scarratt's daughter, in her Sunday best complete with bicycle composes herself while her father takes this photograph of the old castelated gateway to the former Mackworth Castle in 1908. This is the only remnant of a castle erected between 1495 and 1500 and belonging to the Mackworth family. *FWS 211*

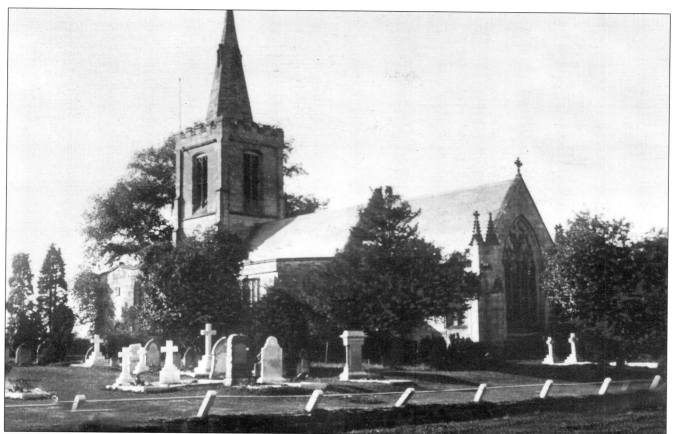

Mackworth. This *c.*1911 view shows the stone building of All Saints' Church, consisting of chancel, nave, south porch with parvise aisles, vestry and a fine battlemented tower surmounted by a short octagonal spire. Much of the original fourteenth-century fabric was restored in 1851. The window of the south aisle displayed in stained glass the various impalements of arms of the Mundy family of Markeaton from the time of Edward I. There are many memorials and tombs relating to the Mundys. *FWS 559*

Markeaton Recreation Ground. In 1910, Scarratt captured typical Edwardian summer weekend scenes at Markeaton Recreation Ground (shown here and on page 89). The fascination of water is obvious as some prefer to paddle whilst others attempt a spot of fishing (and not a bathing costume in sight). The grounds of about nine acres between Ashbourne and Kedleston Roads were presented by F.N.Mundy Esq of Markeaton Hall in 1895 and were opened on 22 October that year. The adjacent Mundy Pleasure Grounds of four and a half acres were presented in 1903 by Mrs F.N.Mundy and were officially opened on 21 June 1905. *FWS 336*

Left: Markeaton. These *c.*1912 scenes are around the well known old wooden bridge across Markeaton Brook. This has been a favourite play area for several generations of Derbeians. The Markeaton Park we know today was not yet in existence (it was opened by the Duke of Kent in 1931). If one looks closely, several members of FWS's family are in each view. *FWS 667*

Another view of Edwardian children enjoying themselves at Markeaton Recreation Ground.

Mickleover. The following three scenes were all coloured unnumbered illustrations of 1906. The first is of Cackle Hill, 'Cackle' possibly being a derivation of 'Cattle'. In this somewhat empty scene looking up Cackle Hill (now Vicarage Road), the farm buildings and old cart possibly belong to the local farming family, Wain.

Mickleover Church. The stone building of All Saints' Church. It consists of chancel, nave, aisles, south porch, vestry and a low embattled western tower with pinnacles, containing a clock and three bells. A new porch was built in 1858 and the Norman church restored.

Mickleover. A somewhat indistinct illustration of the Market Place. The old man with walking stick is close to the old stone drinking fountain. The former family butcher's shop of W.Poyser is on the left of centre with Alfred William Hill's bakery next door (to the right with large door).

Mickleover. This is an extremely scarce photograph taken in 1924 of Chain Lane with the old white cottage to the left. Chain Lane takes its name from the former chains placed across it during the eighteenth century to prevent people from avoiding their toll payments. It was formerly known as Mill Lane, after the windmill which stood on a site approximately where the present Trust House Forte Hotel (Crest) is in what was formerly a house known as the Coppice, which name was also given to the first hotel usage on the site. Chain Lane links Mickleover to Littleover, from Uttoxeter Road to Burton Road, and some readers may feel that this view should have been included with Littleover. *FWS 1146*

Ockbrook. This 1906 scene, published as an unnumbered coloured card, shows the top of the hill looking down Green Lane, Ockbrook. The main road to Derby and Ilkeston is at the bottom. On the lower left, set back behind the white building, is the Royal Oak public house. The row of cottages to the right still exists and contains a newsagent's, Ockbrook News. To the left is Home Farm Close (named after the farm which has disappeared) and which contains modern bungalows.

Ockbrook. This *c.*1908 Abbey Street publication shows the old Moravian lecture hall at the Ockbrook Settlement. Scarratt's pedal cycle is by the right wall. The last cow is entering the gate on the left. *FWS 209*

Ockbrook. The stone building of All Saints' Church in *c.*1911 with its western tower and low octagonal spire (restored 1894). The church itself was restored in 1898 by E.Elsey Esq of Hopwell Hall and a new organ was installed in 1928. *FWS 494*

Ockbrook. Another Scarratt view showing a close up of All Saints' Church as three locals pose in their Sunday best on Church Street in *c.*1911. It was a stone building consisting of chancel, nave, and a tower containing three bells. *FWS 499*

Ockbrook. A sunny scene in *c.*1911 outside the ancient thatched barn in Bare Lane. The small boy with the unusually large white hat appears to be holding newspapers. A garage now stands on the approximate site of the old barn. *FWS 496*

Ockbrook. A distant view of Ockbrook and All Saints' Church taken from Carr Hill during World War One c.1915. This lane is better known as Cole Lane. Carr Hill House is on the right out of view. *FWS 1012*

Ockbrook. The area close to the lych-gates of All Saints' Church in this *c.*1926 illustration appears to be a favourite play area for local children on Church Street. Note the rickety old tricycle. The White Swan public house, advertising Alton's Ales, is tucked away on the right of the picture. *FWS 1302*

Ockbrook. A settlement for Moravians was originally founded here in *c.*1750 and comprised of boarding schools for about 60 boys and 40 girls (this later became 100 girls only) with a chapel seating about 350 people. It became an independent girls' public school and was recognised as such by the Ministry of Education. Both these illustrations were published from Scarratt's Abbey Street premises, so they must be *c.*1908-09. Despite the closeness of their numbers, it is obvious from the growth of the trees and bushes that a significant time period has elapsed between them being taken. A number of trees were demolished to make way for the extension clearly shown in the second view. The gate posts appear to have fallen into disarray. The first illustration (250) was also issued as postcard number 757. *FWS 250 & 252*

Ockbrook. A fine early 1930s view of Church Street showing the Post Office and grocery shop of H.Plant on the corner. The chevron sign for the school is on the bottom left. Note the large rainwater barrels at the front of the cottages on the left. The cottages have now been replaced by modern housing. *FWS 1615*

Quarndon. The original church/chapel of Quarndon, anciently annexed to Derby's All Saints' Church, was a building in the Norman style 44ft x 15ft high with a good Norman south doorway. The only portion of the old church now remaining is the tower covered with ivy, pictured here *c.*1912-13. In the nineteenth century it was in the care of the Revd Joseph Pickford, son of the eminent Derby architect. *FWS 1206*

Quarndon. A gentleman complete with umbrella and straw boater and believed to be none other than Frank Scarratt himself composes himself for this *c.*1908 close-up of the new St Paul's Church erected in 1874 by Giles & Brookhouse. It is of the Early English style, consisting of chancel, nave of four bays, aisles, south porch and an embattled western tower with a short octagonal spire. *FWS 231*

Quarndon. Bunker's Hill, shown here in *c.*1911, with its mounds and three old trees was a popular tourist spot for picnics and courting couples and was situated about 1½ miles from Duffield's old castle. Scarratt's son Alec is in the foreground complete with school cap. In *c.*1862 the site of a Norman pottery kiln was found together with several specimens of important pottery. *FWS 477*

Quarndon. The Black House, a well known landmark in Quarndon for approximately 100 years, is seen here covered in ivy *c.*1910. Seven young ladies, possibly from Lord Scarsdale's endowed school, pose for FWS in the nearby lane next to his motorbike. The man with goggles resting on the left is Scarratt's travelling companion from the firm of Wildt & Kray, whilst those on the right are members of Scarratt's family. *FWS 323*

Quarndon. A little boy (possibly FWS's son Alec) can be seen here in 1910 sitting in the field close to the quaint thatched cottage. The grand timber-fronted house to the left is that of Alfred Jacobson on Quarndon Hill. *FWS 346*

Quarndon. This view in 1910 looking up Church Road towards the Common was one of Scarratt's first publications from his newly acquired premises at 115 Normanton Road. The spire of St Paul's Church can be seen behind the old Wesleyan Chapel built in 1859 (now a high class local provisions store). The row of cottages on the right exists today. *FWS 400*

Quarndon. This 1910 view is looking down Church Road towards Allestree and features the well stocked small front garden adjacent to the front of the ivy-clad Joiner's Arms public house. At one time Quarndon was extensively visited for its chalybeate waters (situated further down beyond the gas lamp). However, the precious waters eventually dried up. *FWS 401*

Quarndon. A typical FWS 1913 five-panel multi-view featuring different views along Church Road, The Common and Bunker's Hill. *FWS 737*

Spondon. The following three illustrations are from Scarratt's 1907 blue print period. The first, above, is of an unusual almost round thatched lodge which was situated on the Derby-Nottingham road and was thought to date to 1785. One theory is that it was a lodge house to the Wilmot family of Spondon Hall, whilst others claim it was a forwarding station where local mail was dropped and collected for distribution to the village of Spondon. We know that in 1820 a lady called Mary Brown lived in this house with its gothic style windows and crumbling stucco facia. The lodge was demolished in 1929, and sometime later a small sub branch of what became the NatWest Bank was built on the site (now closed). To the right is the beginning of Lodge Lane leading uphill to Spondon village and is often referred to as Spondon Lane End. This was also issued as postcard number 216. *FWS 105*

Spondon. Lodge Lane, a busy thoroughfare today but shown here in 1907, was obviously a popular spot for cyclists. They are on the upper portion of Lodge Lane approaching the right turn into Sitwell Street. The gap in the wall on the left near the telegraph pole leads to the church. The house on the right, at one time Dr Tully's, was demolished to be replaced by bungalows. *FWS 106*

Spondon. This church was formerly dedicated to St Mary but was discovered in 1890 to be dedicated to St Werburgh. It is a large stone building chiefly in the Decorated style, consisting of chancel, nave of three bays, aisles, north porch and embattled western tower with spire 114ft high. The church was thoroughly restored in 1892. *FWS 107*

Spondon. Up to ten local children gather around Scarratt's Douglas motor bike in *c*.1914. The enamel sign on the left denotes the Post Office, which later became Mr Kirby's hardware shop (now a cheesery). The Methodist Chapel, built in 1877, with its railings and bracket lamp is on the right. It ceased to be a chapel in 1934 and was for a time an annex to Spondon House School (1930-40). It later became a furniture store workshop, but following fire damage it was refurbished to become the Jehovah's Witnesses' Kingdom Hall. This view is taken from the village looking towards Locko Park and Hall. The large house on the right is Bowes House. *FWS 836*

Scarratt's Derbyshire Scenes

Ambergate. This was one of Scarratt's early 1906 coloured illustrations taken from Ambergate Woods near the present youth hostel looking towards the famous triangular Ambergate Station. The white station master's house is in the middle distance. *FWS 91*

Ambergate. This distant view taken in *c.*1930s from the top of Holly Lane shows the sleepy hillside village of Ambergate, including the former Toadmoor hamlet. The outline of housing on Newbridge Road is top right and Turnbull Hill (top left) can be seen. The former station buildings are on the bottom left. *FWS 1453*

Ambergate. This magnificent house pictured *c.*1930 with beautiful ornate features and gothic tower now lies in ruins awaiting demolition. It was the former home of Thewlis Johnson who acquired it in 1874 from Mr Hurt, whose family owned all the land in the vicinity of Ambergate. He lived here at Oakhurst for the next 22 years, employing a butler, footman, maids and a host of gardeners and grooms. He opened his Ambergate wire works on 22 May 1876. Oakhurst has had many uses since – a Diocesan 'retreat house' during the 1920s and at one time housed self-contained flats. *FWS 1451*

Ambergate. This *c.*1930 scene shows the former Post Office at the junction of Toadmoor Lane and Devonshire Street. The half-timbered black and white building on the main Matlock Road is the popular village watering hole the White House public house. The two round gate posts (bottom left) are the former toll gate posts from the Ambergate Toll Bar (Cromford and Belper Turnpike Trust) which used to span the main Ambergate-Matlock road (the A6) in the vicinity of the Hurt Arms Hotel. The present Little Chef is built close to the site of the old toll house. *FWS 1454*

Ambergate. A leafy *c.*1930 view of the stone arched railway bridge over the River Amber, with a steam train just crossing over on its way north. *FWS 1458*

Ashbourne. A young boy on horseback *c.*1911 outside St Oswald's Church. Dating back to 1241 the church's tower and soaring spire – 212ft in height – dominate the market town of Ashbourne. The spire, ribbed with ball flower ornaments, dates from the fourteenth century and, pierced with 20 dormer lights in five tiers of four each, is a work of great beauty and was known as the 'Pride of the Peak'. The church contains the tombs of the Cokayne, Boothby and Bradburne families. The ornate gothic style stone gate posts and wrought-iron gates were a magnificent site. *FWS 463*

Clifton. The small parish of Clifton was formed in 1846 out of Ashbourne. The War Memorial to local men who died in World War One is shown here in *c.*1930 in the specially walled area. *FWS 1429*

Aston-on-Trent. A horse and cart gently passes All Saints' Church in *c.*1909. The church was built from local stone consisting of chancel with north aisle, clerestorised nave of three bays, aisles and south porches and an embattled western tower with pinnacles. It contains memorials to the Shuttleworth and Holden families. *FWS 289*

Aston-on-Trent. This later view of All Saints', Aston-on-Trent, shows the later addition of the fine lych-gates. The photograph was taken in the mid 1920s. Scarratt's bike is to the right. *FWS 1191*

Aston-on-Trent. This view is of the west front entrance to Aston Hall was photographed in *c.*1915. FWS's motor bike is parked at the entrance to the right of the ionic columns of the porch. The architect was thought to be Richard Leaper. The Hall was the property and residence of Major William Dickson Winterbottom JP. A two-storey extension was added in 1907. The Hall was later turned into a special hospital. *FWS 1005*

Aston-on-Trent. The Hall's neatly laid out walled garden *c.*1912 with an abundance of tulip varieties and garden ornaments was aptly named the 'Dutch Garden'. *FWS 650*

Aston-on-Trent. This view of Aston Lodge was taken *c.*1914. The substantial gate posts supported an intricate and fine wrought iron overmantel and gates designed by the famous Robert Bakewell. The Lodge was demolished some considerable time later and the gates resited to a park in Long Eaton. *FWS 958*

Aston-on-Trent. This *c.*1913 publication is another typical FWS five-panel multi-view, showing the Post Office, the Hall, Weston Road, the Church and the Green. *FWS 738*

Beeley. In this quiet *c.*1911 view of Chapel Street, Beeley, the old Wesleyan Chapel, built in 1890, stands at the top left of the street. The thatched corner house on the left was the refreshment rooms. The house on the right was a superb edifice of stone and ornate features. *FWS 522*

Beeley. Beeley was a small township and parish formed out of Bakewell on the east bank of the River Derwent. Scarratt has captured a tranquil sunny morning *c.*1911 at Brookside, not too far from the Devonshire Arms public house. One can almost hear the water trickling by. *FWS 523*

Beeley. The church of St Anne, shown here in *c*.1911, is an ancient stone building consisting of chancel, nave, south porch and embattled western tower. Memorial windows to William 7th Duke of Devonshire and to Lord Cavendish were provided. The church was extensively restored in 1882-84. The remains of a fine old yew tree existed in the churchyard. *FWS 524*

Belper. This *c*.1909 view was taken from the vicinity of the Triangle looking towards Ashbourne and Belper Lane End. The large jubilee clock tower on the left was erected at the Belper West Mill by the Strutt family in 1897 to celebrate Queen Victoria's Diamond Jubilee. The clock tower was 115ft high and the large clock face (9ft in diameter) was without numbers. The ivy-clad gangway with its gun embrasures (ready to ward off rioters like the Luddites, but never used) forms an arch across the road. The clock tower and mills on the west side and south mill were all demolished in the 1950s. *FWS 275*

Belper. The Market Place was stone paved by George Henry Strutt in 1881. By 1887 it was surrounded by nine public houses and at the rear of the market stalls on the left stood the Angel Inn where a foul murder was once committed. It is difficult to tell, but it looks as if the Edwardian children are possibly at the striped market stalls after they have closed for the day, *c.*1909. A small market is still held here today, but is rapidly diminishing. *FWS 276*

Belper. This is Bridge Street looking up towards the Triangle and Belper Mill in *c.*1909. The young butcher's boy (left) stands in the doorway of James Beresford's shop (now Collector's Choice shop). There was another Beresford family business of marble and granite merchants nearby. The pillared entrance porch to John William Ashton's George Hotel is on the left. Scarratt's pedal cycle is parked on the right. Where the railings are on the right stood the former Savings Bank (now the Clusters Art Gallery). The next building with the two upper bay windows is that of Henry Gillett plumbers, who fitted Herbert Strutt's school out for plumbing, heating, gas fitting and sanitary engineering. The children on the pavement on the right are just passing what is now known as Piggy Hill (formerly called George Place.) *FWS 277*

Belper. Two Edwardian children on their way down Derby Road stop for Scarratt's photograph of Herbert Strutt's Higher Elementary School at midday in 1910. The gothic style building was chiefly constructed using local stone from the Strutt quarry at Makeney. Designs were by the Belper firm of Messrs Hunter & Woodhouse, whilst the builder was J.K.Ford of Derby. The cost was £15,000 and the school was opened on 8 May 1909 by the Duke of Devonshire. It contained a central hall, nine class rooms, art room, laboratories and dining hall, and would accommodate 210 scholars and 30 pupil teachers. There was also a cookery and manual training centre. Over the years the school gained in reputation for its achievements. In 1974 it became a middle school but by 1986 it was a junior and infants school only. *FWS 349*

Brailsford. This is an early 1907 brown print of All Saints' Church, Brailsford. The church is situated equidistant from the villages of Ednaston and Brailsford. The stone Norman style building consists of chancel, nave, south aisle, south porch and a lofty embattled tower at the west end, parts of which date back to the fourteenth and sixteenth century. The church was partially restored in 1862 when a vestry was added; full restoration was completed in 1886. The message on the back of the card reads: 'I have been to the band of hope meeting every week.' *FWS 104*

Breaston. Scarratt's son Alec stands on the right of Duck Lane, Breaston. In this *c.*1912-13 view the road surface is largely unmade, puddled and without pavements, but is much improved today. *FWS 775*

Coxbench. The white painted wooden level crossing gates are closed across the Ripley branch of the Midland Railway, and the tall wooden semaphore signal stands at danger. The crossing house with its interesting brickwork and ornate gables, seen here in 1910, is now a private residence. The young boy on the fence is Scarratt's son Alec. *FWS 378*

Coxbench. Anciently called St Anthony's Cross, Coxbench is a hamlet half a mile south of Holbrook and was partly in Horsley parish and partly in Holbrook township. This *c*.1914 view is looking towards Horsley and shows the old cottages on the east side of the slip road to Horsley, called Horsley Lane, accessed under the present A38 bridge. *FWS 844*

Coxbench. A pony and trap have just passed the old station house (top right). The black and white half-timbered facia of the Fox and Hounds public house complete with stable door is on the left. The man in cloth cap and waistcoat in this *c*.1914 view is probably William Haynes, who was the landlord at that time. The pub sign does not appear to exist at this time. *FWS 949*

Coxbench. This *c.*1908 green print shows the somewhat dilapidated Mrs Gray's thatched cottage at Coxbench, situated just before the Fox and Hounds public house. The adjacent cottages are shown in varying degrees of collapse. Could that be young Mrs Gray leaning on the wall with white bonnet in front of her cottage? Mrs Scarratt's bike is parked in the right foreground. *FWS 183*

Darley Dale. A small boy in white jacket and cap stands by the magnificent gate posts and iron gates leading to St Helen's Church in Darley Dale. On this sunny afternoon in *c.*1911 Scarratt has parked his motor bike (complete with front satchel and rear wooden saddle box) against the churchyard wall. The cruciform church of St Helen's, dating from the twelfth century, consists of chancel, clerestoried nave of four bays, transepts, south porch and western tower containing a clock and eight bells. In the south transept is a monument to Sir John de Darley whose family held the royal manor of Darley in the thirteenth century. The church was restored in 1877 at a cost of over £3,000. The churchyard contained a very old yew tree 323ft in girth at 4ft from the ground. *FWS 453*

Darley Dale. The Whitworth Institute was erected in 1890 by the philanthropy of the late Sir Joseph Whitworth Baronet FRS. It comprised of reading room, library, museum, swimming bath and billiard room. Attached to the institute were large pleasure grounds, and playing fields complete with an ornamental lake for boating. The nine young ladies in this *c.*1936 view appear to be enjoying their respective boat trips. The lake has since been filled in. *FWS 1686*

Denby. Smithy Houses is a small hamlet one and a half miles south-west of Denby. Denby was noted for its extensive collieries, which were the property of Captain William Drury-Lowe JP. There were also large blast furnaces in the vicinity for the production of pig iron belonging to the Denby Iron & Coal Co Ltd. In this *c.*1912 scene taken opposite the Smithy Houses Post Office and grocery shop of John Cresswell (left), the Denby Colliery chimney and furnace are visible in the middle distance. A chicken quietly pecks away at the roadside near Scarratt's 'trademark' motor bike. The quietness is about to be disturbed by the local colliery brass band outside the three-storey building of the Drury Arms Hotel on the right. The hotel was then run by Mrs R.Ellen Fletcher. *FWS 677*

Denby. This *c.*1912 view taken from the south-east shows Denby's church of St Mary the Virgin which stands in the centre of the village. The fabric is thirteenth and fifteenth century. It consists of chancel, clerestoried nave, aisles, south porch and a decorated western tower of three stages with a parapet from within which rises a spire with two rows of dormer lights. The fourteenth-century tower supports a broached tower founded by the Rosels. The church has memorials to the Drury-Lowe family of Locko Park. A memorial stone to Thomas Headley, eldest son of Timothy Briggs, died 1895 aged 28 years, is clearly visible in the left foreground of the churchyard. *FWS 678*

Denby. The Vicarage was built in 1904 from designs by Messrs Hunter & Woodhouse, the architects in Belper, who also designed Herbert Strutt's School at Belper. Originally the Vicarage, including 33 acres of glebe land, were the gift of Captain John Alfred Edwin Drury-Lowe JP. Scarratt's familiar motor bike R711 is parked against the stone wall in this *c.*1912 scene. *FWS 679*

Denby. In this *c.*1912 scene the young Midland Railway servant has just closed the old wooden level crossing gates to the road in readiness for a train arriving at Denby Station on the Ripley branch line. The station master was C.J.Reynall. It is believed Frank Scarratt and his wife Mary are on the platform ramp on the right. *FWS 681*

Draycott. This somewhat faded view is an early 1907 Scarratt original photograph looking up Station Road, Draycott, towards Nottingham. It was eventually printed abroad and issued as one of his early brown wash style coloured publications number 142. On the immediate left is the old chemist's shop of Wathes & Jackson which later became Ed Bassett Flemon's chemist's shop (and eventually Thomas Brierley's). The horse-drawn cab in the distant left is opposite the premises of Francis Perks & Son who were builders and contractors. Next door is the ornate Victorian iron pillared porch of William Topham's grocery and drapers store. This beautiful porch is still in existence but the store is now an antique shop. *FWS 142*

Draycott. This *c.*1913 view looking down Victoria Road, Draycott, has two young cyclists in the immediate foreground. They are Scarratt's children Winnie and Alec, who also appear in the scene below on Derby Road. The Victoria Hotel stands on the left-hand side, hidden by the overhanging trees. William North's greengrocery shop is the corner shop on the middle right-hand side. *FWS 653*

Draycott. A sunny day has brought many children out to play on Derby Road, Draycott, in this *c.*1913 view, Scarratt's children with their bikes again are to the right. The advertising hoarding on the left is promoting Immingham as 'England's latest port'. *FWS 655*

Draycott. This mid-1920s scene shows several children outside Theodore R.Fritchley's butcher's shop complete with advertising awning on Victoria Road, Draycott. The unusual 'Moorish' shaped clock tower of the Victoria Lace Mill, built in 1907, is visible in the distance. It was the property of Messrs Jardine of Nottingham. The Primitive Methodist Chapel can be seen on the right and appears to be partially artist drawn. *FWS 1279*

Duffield. The *c.*1913 view of Little Eaton Bank, Duffield, shows the Bridge Inn public house on the left with the country lane ambling towards Little Eaton in the distance. The small lane on the right between the two hedges eventually leads down to Duffield Church. This photographic postcard was produced by Scarratt for Jas Henry Stapleton's Post Office in Town Street, Duffield. FWS's bike is parked against the old gas lamp. *FWS 796*

Elvaston. This double view postcard was published by Scarratt *c.*1910 from his Abbey Street premises. The lofty tower of St Bartholomew's Church, which stands close to Elvaston Castle, is on the left, and consists of chancel, clerestoried nave, south aisle, south porch, north transept forming a memorial chapel of the Stanhope family, and a western tower with pinnacles. This church was extensively rebuilt in 1474, and later restored throughout in 1904 by G.F.Boldey Esq RA. It contains memorials to Sir John Stanhope and the 3rd Earl of Harrington. On the right is Elvaston Castle, showing two smiling Edwardian girls (probably Scarratt's daughters) at the entrance, with the archway and clock tower above. It was the seat of the Earl of Harrington and was built in the domestic gothic style standing in a well wooded park of about 140 acres, containing a lake. The Elvaston Castle estate is now a country park of some 200 acres. *FWS unnumbered*

Elvaston. Scarratt took this view of Elvaston Castle's well laid out Italian gardens during the mid-1920s. They were a handsome sight with their hand-cut dome bushes and white marble statues. In 1895 the compiler of *Bulmers Directory on Derby and Area* wrote: 'The grounds were formerly a triumph of landscape gardening, but they are now shorn of their beauty and the Italian gardens, except for its statuary is no longer worthy of its name.' At one time up to 90 gardeners were employed on the estate. It was in 1830 when the 4th Earl of Harrington appointed William Barron to lay out the grounds (Capability Brown refused the commission). This illustration was published from 28 Green Lane, only the third issue from this address so far found. *FWS 1287*

Etwall. This is an unnumbered early 1908 production showing the centre of Etwall facing Church Hill. It looks as if some of the cloth-capped figures to the right of the picture have just paid a visit to the cycle shop of John Sanders which was situated close to the Spread Eagle public house (note the large inn sign hanging from a post).

Etwall. A somewhat empty looking Derby Road scene in early 1908 looking from the Hawk and Buckle public house towards Derby. FWS's bike is parked alongside the first white house on the right. *FWS 225*

Etwall. It was a bright day in 1911 when FWS parked his bike on the left in order to take this Egginton Road scene. It was in this vicinity that the marl pit or marlow was situated (an early repository site before linkage with the town sewer). The former primary school and workhouse were situated nearby. *FWS 422*

Etwall. The almshouses pictured here in 1912 were initially completed by Sir John Port, who in 1556 devised lands for the foundation and endowment of an almshouse for 16 poor persons and a grammar school at Repton. In 1681 the number of almsmen was doubled. In the 1980s the then ancient flatlets were replaced by eight up-to-date two-storey units and 12 flats. The entrance gates of Etwall Hall (previously the seat of the Port and Cotton families) by the noted Derby blacksmith Robert Bakewell were re-erected in front of the almshouses in 1984. *FWS 669*

Etwall. This interior view of St Helen's Church, Etwall, was taken in 1913. It contains an ornate stone gospel desk or lectern, (right) a reading desk dated 1635 existed in the Port Chapel. It contains monuments of Sir John Port who gave his name to the local school; he was also the founder of Etwall Hospital. *FWS 766*

Etwall. This is one of the last photographs Scarratt took before his retirement in the late 1930s. This view of Derby Road was taken from the church tower. The Hawk and Buckle Inn, complete with archway to its car park, is in the centre and was originally owned by the Cotton family and dates back to 1804. It was sold to Thompson's (later Marston's) Brewery in 1890. The landlord in the late 1920s was Ernest Stephen Laver. The small shop to the left of the large house on the right had a sign above the window 'L.Wain'. The Post Office is just visible on the extreme right. *FWS 1837*

Findern. This view of All Saints', Findern, was published as a *c.*1906 coloured postcard. The church is in the Early English style consisting of chancel, south porch, nave, north aisle and a western tower with spire containing a clock and two bells dated 1841 and 1704 respectively. The church was erected in 1863 to replace an ancient chapel. *FWS 88*

Haddon Hall, *c.*1911. A very fine and complete specimen of an ancient baronial residence, Haddon Hall stands on an acclivity on the eastern bank of the River Wye. The tower of the gateway is supposed to have been built in the reign of Edward III. One of the most ancient parts of the structure, dating from 1427, is the chapel. Dorothy Vernon eloped with (and was later married to in particularly romantic circumstances) Sir John Manners, the second son of Thomas, 1st Earl of Rutland KG. Subsequently Haddon became the property of the Dukes of Rutland. It was the principal seat of that family until the beginning of the eighteenth century. *FWS 520*

Heanor. A view looking down the High Street, Heanor, in 1913. The Post Office and shipping agents office of Mr Thomas Ball is on the right adjacent to the gas lamp post at 20 High Street. The adjacent corner building selling Shipstones Ales is the local off-licence or beer retailers. The large double-gabled imposing building on the left is that of I.R.Morley hosiery manufacturer, built in 1874. Mrs Scarratt is standing on the adjacent pavement with FWS's car further down on the left, while his daughter is in the left foreground. *FWS 724*

Heanor. Looking down Market Street in early 1913 towards the High Street, obviously before the tram lines were laid. The Red Lion public house is in the distance at the junction leading to Smalley and Derby. At the top right stands the Heanor Observer printers premises and Poole's the bootmaker. On the left is the framing shop of Frederick Mason and the Foster Brothers outfitters at 25 Market Street. *FWS 725*

Heanor. Mrs F.W.Scarratt and son, in a rare close-up, smile for Frank outside the new Heanor Technical School in 1913, not too long after it was erected in 1912 at a cost of £15,000. The old technical school was at Heanor Hall and was demolished in 1910 so that the above purpose-built school could be constructed on the same site. Two of the old hall's trees were left *in situ* to the front. This is now part of the South East Derbyshire College. *FWS 726*

Heanor. Two local lads pose for FWS in the morning sun alongside the wall in this 1913 view looking down Mansfield Road. Mrs Scarratt again appears on the right-hand side. The Revd Cyril Hankin-Turvin BA, curate of All Saints' Church, Marlpool, lived on this road, as did Revd William Henry Hopkin BA, the curate of St Lawrence Church, Heanor (previously dedicated to St Michael). *FWS 728*

Holbrook. This is Holbrook village centre in *c*.1911 looking towards Belper. The little girl in the distant left has just passed the Spotted Cow public house. Scarratt's trusty motor bike is parked on the left against the side of the Greyhound pub. At this time the pub was in the hands of Messrs Thomas Walker and Samuel Ward. A sign over the door (out of view left) used to state: 'House of the Derbyshire Public House Trust Company Ltd. Samuel Ward, licensed victualler, manager. Tea and refreshments always provided. Licensed to sell Tobacco. (Closed on Sundays).' It has now reverted to being a private residence. The old corner shop in the distant left is now the delightful Gas Light Gallery belonging to the artistic Charles Forster. It was formerly R.M.Bailey's grocer's shop. *FWS 566*

Holbrook. A local farmer leads his horse up Mellor's Lane, Holbrook, past the magnificent tree on the right. Scarratt's son Alec is sitting in the triangle of grass that appears to have been purposely cultivated as part of the road. This *c*.1915 scene is from Church Street but there appears to be nothing remaining of the view today. *FWS 1037*

Holbrook. Four cute little local children, one with a bunch of flowers, pose for FWS in Moor Pool Lane, Holbrook, *c*.1915. Scarratt's son, by the wall on the right, has again followed his nomadic father on his photographic mission. This is now called Pond Road, and the large house has had to make way for our modernised world. *FWS 1039*

Holbrook. Scarratt's Douglas motor bike is wheeled away to the house on the left called The Crofts (which still exists today). This *c*.1915 photograph is looking down Moorside Lane towards Holbrook village centre from the junction with Chapel Street. Local children play on the right whilst looking at Francis Scarratt who is standing in the road on the right (so who took the photograph?). *FWS 1040*

Holbrook. This *c.*1915 view of Holbrook Moor is taken from the vicinity of The Wheel public house (surprisingly, this drinking establishment is not listed in either *Kelly's Derby* directories for 1912 or 1928). The building on the left where Scarratt's son is sitting has long since gone. The small children in the distant right are outside a former beer retailer's house which later became the Cross Keys public house. A newsagent's shop now exists on the bottom left-hand corner and the lane is now called Chapel Street. *FWS 1041*

Holbrook. St Michael's Church, Holbrook, seen here in 1911, was originally erected in 1761 by the Revd S.Bradshaw as a private chapel for Holbrook Hall. It was eventually consecrated as the Parish Church in 1835 and enlarged and partly rebuilt in 1842 by the late William Evans Esq MP of Allestree. The building is of stone in the Italian style consisting of nave, north and south porches and a western turret containing one bell. It was thoroughly renovated in 1887-88 and reseated by Sir Thomas W.Evans and others. On the Sunday evening of 27 January 1907, a disastrous fire destroyed a great part of the interior. It was restored and a new south aisle added and a chancel created. The floor of the chancel is of marble and Hopton stone. *FWS 562*

Holbrook. This delightful leafy lane scene *c.*1915 is looking down Coxbench Lane, Holbrook. This lane eventually comes out at the bottom of the road which leads to the Railway Station and level crossing. The boy on the right has managed a smile for the group of young girls coming up the lane. *FWS 1050*

Holbrook. This view shows the grand double-gabled convalescent home complete with its central clock tower *c.*1910. It was the convalescent home of the Derbyshire Royal Infirmary and was erected in 1899 and contained 28 beds. It was a fine building of stone with well laid out grounds. Miss M.Holland was the matron during this period and later a Miss Tyrrel. It later became the headquarters of the Derbyshire County Nursing Association which had 93 nursing associations affiliated to it in the various towns and villages of Derbyshire. The president was the Duchess of Devonshire. *FWS 350*

Holbrook. This grand ivy-clad residence with its gothic style turret was that of Joseph Bourne Wheeler Esq JP in 1911. The house was called Nether Lea. The following illustration shows the garden steps leading to the tennis court. *FWS 564 & FWS 1051*

Holbrook. A typical Scarratt five-panel multi-view of Holbrook showing Coxbench Lane, the village (2), Nether Lea, and convalescent home. *FWS 740*

Horsley. This view from the village fountain looking up to St Clement's Church, Horsley is *c*.1907 and was originally issued as one of Scarratt's brown wash prints number 182. The distinctive lofty broach spire can be seen for miles around. The house roof on the left was probably once thatched and in this view, it has been patched up with corrugated iron sheeting. The lady drawing water into her bucket from the ornate fountain was a well-known local character. The fountain, complete with embossed gargoyle lion style heads, is inscribed 'The Sophia 1864'. A castle, built in the thirteenth century, formerly stood here but has long since been destroyed. *FWS 711*

Horsley. This ornate oval, published in colour, contains a 1910 view of St Clement's Church, Horsley, which is seated conspicuously on a height. It consists of chancel, clerestoried nave, aisles with arcades of three bays and a western tower and spire containing a clock and five bells. The tower dates from the fourteenth century and was greatly altered c.1405, and restored in 1858-60. In 1898 the spire was repaired and a lightning conductor added at a cost of £70. *FWS 199*

Horsley Woodhouse. This c.1912 photograph shows the unspoilt view of the Sitwell Arms public house at Horsley Woodhouse. The landlord at this time was Mr Samuel Brooks. The ecclesiastical parish was formed in 1878 from the parish of Horsley. The area has many connections with Robert Sacheverell Wilmot Sitwell Esq of Stainsby House, who was lord of the manor and principal landowner, hence the pub name. The front of the building has been somewhat spoilt in appearance by a modern extension. *FWS 700*

Hulland. The village of Hulland is delightfully seated on an eminence three and a half miles west from Shottle Station. By Local Government Board order, a detached part of Turnditch was in 1886 transferred from Turnditch to Hulland township. The population in 1901 was only 214. However, the population of Hulland ecclesiastical parish in 1901 was 622. This serene scene of the Green looking towards Ashbourne was taken *c*.1912. It is now the A517 road. The fine ivy-clad house on the right was believed to be the residence of Robert Walker. It is now called Hulland Nurseries and also offers bed and breakfast and cream teas. *FWS 683*

Hulland. The small stone building of Christ Church, Hulland, pictured here in *c*.1912, was erected in 1838. It consists of a nave and an embattled western tower containing one bell. There were 273 sittings, all being free. The vicar since 1911 was the Revd William James Dannatt MA of Queen's College, Cambridge. *FWS 685*

Hulland. Scarratt's motor bike rests against the white wooden rails as he takes this view looking towards Ashbourne, of the Hollow, Hulland, in *c*.1913. The bicycle looks a trifle too large for the young boy who has become the focal point for FWS in this scenic part of the lane. The Hollow is approximately 150 yards beyond Hulland Green. The trees on the right have now disappeared; however, the railings denoting the presence of a small brook running under the road are still present in some form today. *FWS 784*

Hulland Ward. By Local Government Board order in 1886, part of Mugginton parish and a detached part of Turnditch were transferred to Hulland Ward township. This *c*.1912 view looking towards Ashbourne shows the saddler's premises of Anthony Beresford Dale. On the immediate left his local shop also advertises Eley Cartridges and Lipton's Teas. A horse has been tethered outside the appropriately named Nag's Head public house (top left). Scarratt's travelling companion is seen with his motor bike standing in the centre of the main road through Wardgate with Scarratt's own bicycle parked on the right. *FWS 686*

Hulland Ward. RB 6108 is parked outside the small village Post Office and shop at Hulland Ward in *c*.1936. Mr Fred Archer was at one time the man in charge here. This view is looking towards Ashbourne. *FWS 1725*

Hulland Ward. This 1936 scene shows Scarratt's Morris car parked outside the Nag's Head public house in the distant left, behind the telegraph pole. Joseph Oakley Jnr was the long-time landlord here. Harry Harvey Dale's saddlers business is on the left. John Willetts' blacksmith's shop stands on the right. *FWS 1726*

Idridgehay. Ireton Wood was a considerable hamlet one mile south-west from Idridgehay Railway Station. Henry Swingler Esq of Edge Hill, Duffield was the principal landowner. This tranquil scene of the lake has been captured *c.*1916 with 'Evelyn' carefully moored at the right-hand side. *FWS 1043*

Idridgehay. This *c.*1936-37 leafy scene off Hillcliffe Lane, Idridgehay, shows the sizeable Sherbourne stream and bridge. The house on the left exists today. The cart tracks appear to indicate that the stream at one time was crossed by horse and cart. *FWS 1775*

Kilburn. The Lodge House or toll bar in this *c.*1911 scene was located on the turnpike road between Ripley and Derby (now the B6179). It was close to the gang road of Outram's railway. The house existed at the junction until the early 1930s when it was demolished to enable the road to be widened. The toll house had the first WC in the area (supposedly a crude plank with hole suspended over the nearby brook). The original stone gate post still exists. A wall letter box was here for many years. *FWS 567*

Kilburn. Many children are evident on Church Street, Kilburn, in this *c.*1913 view. Outside the thatched cottages on the right (both demolished in the 1950s) a road sweeper and Scarratt's bike are visible on the left. To the left of the thatched cottages is the New Mission Room, erected in 1912, being an annex of St Clement's Church at Horsley. It was used for church functions, wedding receptions, whist drives and Scout/Guide meetings. During World War Two it was completely refurbished and became Kilburn Village Hall. *FWS 712*

Kilburn. With R711 safely parked, Scarratt took this fine *c.*1913 photograph of Chapel Street, Kilburn. Most of the young local boys were able to give FWS a large smile. The village shops are in the distant left whilst the old Wesleyan Chapel (1891) is out of the picture to the right. *FWS 713*

Kirk Langley. This is one of Scarratt's early 'ornate border' types *c.*1908. The stone church of St Michael consists of chancel, clerestoried nave, aisles and a low embattled western tower. The church was extensively restored in 1890-91, the lych-gate being added later. The Meynell family have close relations with this church. This view was previously issued as number 103 blue print. *FWS 220*

Kirk Langley. A *c*.1911 view of the crossroads at Kirk Langley. The local gentleman and horse near to Scarratt's bike have probably just returned from the local farrier. The premises of Samuel Clarke, a local baker and provisions dealer, is in the distant left. The old Post Office and telegraph office is just visible behind the telegraph pole. *FWS 480*

Kirk Langley. A quiet rural scene close to the village duck pond on Church Lane in *c*.1914. A pony and trap is visible in the distance. *FWS 839*

Kirk Langley. This view is looking up Derby Road, Kirk Langley, *c*.1914 towards St Michael's Church in the far distance. Scarratt's bike on the right appears to have some sort of coiled tubing across the handlebars. *FWS 840*

Langley Mill. A fine *c*.1913 view looking down Eastwood Lane, Langley Mill. Mary Scarratt stands by the fence on the left. The shoe and boot repair shop on the immediate left advertises 'All best English leather used by experienced workmen'. It is thought that this was probably the premises of Wyles Bros. Ltd, or Strong & Co, both of whom operated in this area. *FWS 722*

Little Eaton. The two farmers, along with their horse and cart, have come from the Coxbench direction and are about to cross over Jack O'Darley Bridge on to the Main Road through Little Eaton *c.*1911. The house in the top left belonged to the well-to-do Brindley family. Messages on postcards often refer to people staying at 'Mount Pleasant' or at 'Mr Brindley's house'. The large house on the bend (right) has obviously been built during the next two or three years, replacing the small stone building from the view below. *FWS 478*

Little Eaton. This *c.*1908 photograph was taken from Jack O'Darley Bridge looking towards Coxbench. Little Eaton stone quarries are visible in the background. They have not been worked for a long time. Mount Pleasant House is just visible top left. *FWS 223*

Little Eaton. This is one of Scarratt's earliest publications, originally being a coloured view of St Paul's Church, Little Eaton, in 1906. It was rebuilt in 1791 in imitation of the Norman style, consisting of chancel, nave, aisles with an arcade of four bays, south porch and an embattled western tower containing one bell. Prior to 1791 this church had lain in a ruinous condition and had temporarily served as a blacksmith's shop. This view is taken from the main road from Little Eaton with the turn to Kilburn on the right. The left turn, now Vicarage Lane, leads to a dead-end towards Park Farm. The building on the left is the parish rooms (formerly the National School) dated 1841 and restored in 1902 by George Herbert Strutt Esq JP. *FWS 87*

Little Eaton. This is a *c.*1911 view of the old toll bar, Little Eaton, which was situated on the main Alfreton Road before demolition due to road widening in the 1920s. The turning on the left is from Duffield where the New Inn public house is situated approximately 150 yards from this junction. The chimney on the left is that of the Brook paper mill belonging to paper manufacturers, Dowdings Ltd. *FWS 434*

Long Eaton. Two young girls smile in the middle of the road at the junction of Main Street and Station Street. The grand new Central premises of the Long Eaton Co-operative Society are situated on the left, and were opened in 1900. Above the shops was the People's Hall which was the largest public meeting place in the district. In this *c*.1911 view there seems to be an unusual amount of water in the road. The tall factory on the right with a finial on the gable was Joseph Orchard's Bank Street lace factory, built in 1881 and destroyed by fire in 1971. *FWS 539*

The High Tor Rock is only 400ft high, but it dominates the gorge between Matlock Bridge and Cromford and perhaps contributes more than any other single object to the peculiarly romantic character of the Matlock scenery. Its upper part is quite perpendicular, and the lower consists of 'screes overgrown with scrub and timber of large dimensions,' according to M.J.B.Baddeley's book of 1883, *The Peak District of Derbyshire*. It is a vast and imposing mass of limestone, beneath which the graceful River Derwent glides along, frequently hidden by the overhanging trees. To the geologists, the High Tor is especially interesting for the fine section of the strata which it exhibits. Near the base a stratum of toadstone intervenes, separating the first and second limestones. Scarratt's travelling companion is on his motor bike, probably his brother Albert on this occasion in 1909. The High Tor Grotto, a natural cavern situated immediately at the base of the cliff from which it derives its name, exhibited splendid groups of crystallised spar and other minerals, lining the roof and sides. It was lit by gas. *FWS 310*

These two typical Scarratt types, show summer time at Trent Lock *c.*1911. Some of the children paddle, whilst others play in the large wooden boats moored to the side. This spot has attracted many visitors over the years. A favourite steamboat called *Erminie* used to travel these waters. In the distance the iron railway bridge and ornate castellated Red Hill Tunnel mouth are just visible. The two-storey wooden boat house with its verandah was a considerable construction. The flag pole was also of a good height. *FWS 541 & 543*

Matlock Bath. This view shows the well-known tunnel and weir at Matlock Bath. The message on the reverse of this *c.*1911 post card reads: 'From Sling Camp, Salisbury, 13.6.17 with love from Archie. Note the break in the railway tunnel.' *FWS 510*

Matlock Bath. This is a fine close-up of Mrs Mary Scarratt, who stands out from the crowd, seen here on the right of Derwent Parade (North Parade) in Matlock Bath *c.*1911. The pub sign on the near top right advertises the George Vaults public house (run by Frank Eato at that time) which is set back through an archway. This archway and yard is now known as the George Centre and the pub has become the nearest thing to a real Italian restaurant you will ever encounter in Derbyshire. Salvatori and his family are renowned for their good food and friendly service. Talk sensible politics here and you could be in for a free Strega. *FWS 509*

Melbourne. This quiet morning scene in *c.*1912 of the Market Place, Melbourne, shows an old man sitting with his dog by the large monument. This, complete with its upper lamp and pump, was erected in 1889, belatedly to mark Queen Victoria's Golden Jubilee of 1887. The ornate Methodist Chapel to the right is a fine gothic stone building erected in 1869. The columned spire was removed after storm damage. The thatched house to the left is the former Nag's Head public house (later replaced by a Co-op building). *FWS 609*

King's Newton. This publication is probably one of the Scarratt Co's last issues (unnumbered and states to rear, Scarratt & Co, Derby). The main feature in this view of the Main Street, King's Newton is the Gayborder Nurseries. At one time the late William Sydenham was in charge, followed by A.H.Harrison. They were horticulturists specialising in hardy garden plants. In the far right of this many gabled building stands the Hardinge Arms public house.

Milford. This view taken from the Rock Quarry, Milford, in late 1910 shows the bridge over the River Derwent and the weirs. Originally the bridge was very narrow and was eventually widened. To achieve this the former toll house (on the end of the bridge corner, towards Makeney) had to be cut in half. In the distance are Fletcher Bros flour mills. The cluster of three buildings on the left include the King William IV public house and chapel. This was previously issued as postcard number 342 and published from Normanton Road, not Abbey Street, presumably in his transitional period between changing premises. *FWS 1010*

Milford. The sweep of terraced houses on the right are all part of Hopping Hill, Milford. The church of Holy Trinity (right) was erected in 1848 in the Early English style on a site given by Messrs Strutt at a cost of £2,000. The church room and vestry were added in 1910. At the junction of Hopping Hill and Matlock Road (now the A6) a stone monument to those who died in World War One was added *c*.1920s. Swainsley Court, a small hamlet (now disappeared), is just visible in the distance. This view of 1915 is looking up the main road (A6) towards Matlock. *FWS 1011*

Morley. The leaf-clad porch to the church of St Matthew's is seen here in *c*.1914. The porch and doorway were thought to have come from Dale Abbey and re-erected here. The nave of the church is Norman and other parts date from the fourteenth century. The stained glass windows contain important medieval glass, some of it being reclaimed after the dissolution of Dale Abbey in 1539. The church contains many memorials to the Sacheveral, Wilmot and Sitwell families. *FWS 950*

Morley. The graceful shaft of this early Saxon cross, complete with its steps and nearly perfect head, stands a little to the west of the church in this *c*.1916 view. The man sitting on the cross steps is non other than Francis William Scarratt himself. Note the hidden additional ornate iron monument covered in ivy to the left. *FWS 1076*

Turnditch. Three cyclists appear at the top of the rise to Turnditch Hill having sensibly decided to walk rather than ride. The public elementary school, pictured here *c*.1913, was erected in 1846 for 110 children. At this time Mr H.Worthy was the master and Miss Ida Gregory was the mistress. *FWS 770*

Weston-on-Trent. Weston-on-Trent Station was situated on the Derby, Castle Donington and Trent branch line of the Midland Railway. The old signal box is visible in the distant right in this *c*.1914 scene. Note the lower quadrant semaphore mechanical signal has been cleared to allow the steam train to pass through the station. Thomas Oldfield, the station master at that time, can be seen in the doorway of the brick platform building. Scarratt's son Alec proudly stands on the other platform for his father's photograph. The station was last used for passenger traffic on 21 September 1928. *FWS 885*

Weston-on-Trent. Scarratt's son can be seen again by the left-hand wall in this 1914 view of Station Corner on Main Street. The Ebenezer Methodist Chapel is behind and was built in 1846. It was used as a rest room at some time during World War Two. *FWS 890*

Weston-on-Trent. This is a *c.*1911 view of the ancient church of St Mary's, Weston-on-Trent. The stone building consists of chancel, nave of three bays, aisles of extreme width, south porch and an embattled western tower with octagonal spire containing three bells. The church was entirely reseated and restored in 1877, and reroofed with oak in 1911 at a cost of £533. Parts of the church are fourteenth century. *FWS 476*

Willington. Another of Scarratt's early blue prints of 1908, showing a horse and cart passing under the centre arch of the railway bridge. Staff from Repton and Willington Station are standing close to the bridge (indistinct). The church of St Michael is just distinguishable in the far distance through the centre arch. *FWS 178*

Wilne. The church of St Chad is situated in Church Wilne, one mile east of Draycott, and dates to the late thirteenth century. The small boy in the churchyard is Scarratt's son Alec on a day out with his father in *c*.1912. It is a stone structure in the Early English style. Fire attacked the church in 1917, destroying the roof and the interior, but it was fully restored in 1923 at a cost of £7,000. It houses what is allegedly the oldest font in England, dated *c*.700. The church now stands in an isolated position, the village retreating to Draycott due to flooding. *FWS 603*

Wilne Village. This 1914 illustration by FWS was sent on a postcard on 1 August 1917 and the message reads: 'The church on the other side is the one that was burnt down.' The lower part of the tower is Early English and the arcade separating the nave and south aisle had to be heavily restored due to fire damage. The old font suffered damage but was skilfully repaired. Strangely, the Wilne cotton mills close to the River Derwent were also destroyed by fire in 1917. *FWS 942*

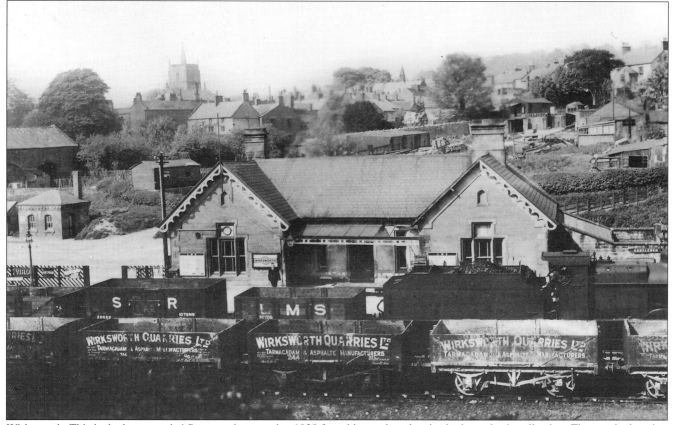

Wirksworth. This is the last recorded Scarratt photograph *c.*1938 from his numbered series in the author's collection. The terminal station is part of the branch line of the Midland Railway from Derby. The fireman can be seen stoking his engine in readiness to take out empty SR & LMS wagons. In the foreground are the wagons advertising Wirksworth Quarries Ltd tar macadam and asphalt manufacturers. The central tower of St Mary's Church with its small lead covered spire can be seen in the distant left. *FWS 1846*

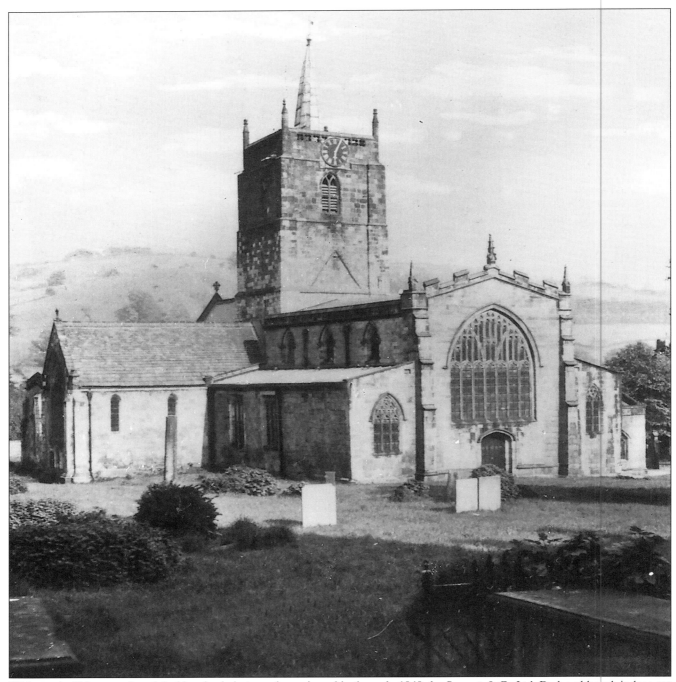

Wirksworth. This unnumbered deckle-edged photograph was issued in the early 1940s by Scarratt & Co Ltd, Derby, although it does not look at all like a Francis Scarratt production. The church of St Mary the Virgin is a cruciform building in the late style of English gothic consisting of chancel with aisles and clerestory transepts, clerestoried nave of three bays, aisles, south porch and central tower with small spire. Monuments to the Gell family of Hopton exist here. Most of the present building dates from the thirteenth, fourteenth and fifteenth centuries.

Outside the County

The nomadic Scarratt also took many photographs outside the county boundary of Derbyshire. The following illustrations cover Leicestershire, Nottinghamshire and Staffordshire. They give an insight only into the several hundred photographs that he produced (mainly of the Staffordshire and Leicestershire areas). It is hoped that at some time in the future, a second book of Scarratt's photographs will be produced covering some of these areas in depth.

Leicestershire

Ashby-de-la-Zouch. This coloured view of the parish church of St Helen's, Ashby-de-la-Zouch, was taken in 1906. The church was restored and enlarged in 1880. There are eight handsome stained windows, the subjects forming a connected history of our Lord's life. *FWS 96*

Ashby-de-la-Zouch. This *c.*1911 photograph shows the castle built in 1480 and now in ruins. It is situated near to the parish church and was for a time the prison of Mary, Queen of Scots. *FWS 530*

Breedon-on-the-Hill. This *c.*1915 scene shows Scarratt's wife 'Polly' and son Alec on the path from the church of St Mary and St Hardulph at Breedon-on-the-Hill. The church is partly Norman and was once part of Breedon Priory founded in 1144 as a cell of St Oswald of Nostell, Yorkshire, for a prior and five canons of the Augustinian order. The north aisle is the private chapel and burial place of the Ferrers family. *FWS 968*

Breedon-on-the-Hill. This north Leicestershire village lies five miles north-east of Ashby-de-la-Zouch. Lime burning was the principal industry. The young boy in this late *c.*1934 illustration is standing adjacent to the unusually shaped round house with its heavy studded door. This was an early punishment house. The Hastings Arms Inn stands to the right. This has now reverted to a private home. *FWS 1644*

Castle Donington. Scarratt's motor bike is parked in the leafy drive leading to Donington Park lodge *c.*1914. Donington Park contained a mansion house in a deer park containing some magnificent oak trees. At one time Selina, Countess of Huntingdon, lived here. Both Charles X of France and poet Tom Moore visited here. The huge complex now forms part of the famous Donington Park race track circuit. *FWS 936*

Castle Donington. This is a 1913 view of St Luke's Church, Castle Donington, built mainly in the Early English style. It has sedilia and piscinae, a squint and two canopied niches outside the south aisle. Some of the piers are octagonal and some have octagonal capitals with dog-tooth ornaments. *FWS 781*

Castle Donington. This is Castle Donington's famous cedar tree shown here in 1913. Many of its branches have had to be supported due to their weight. *FWS 783*

Castle Donington. This World War One view shows the magnificent Donington Hall *c*.1915 surrounded by barbed wire and sentry boxes. Prisoners-of-war such as German naval officers were held here. *FWS 1021*

Castle Donington. A typical *c.*1913 multi-view production showing Ashby Road, High Street, Market Street, Hemington and Old Farm. *FWS 739*

Castle Donington. This is a late 1930s multi-view production showing Old Cedar, Hemington Church, the Hall and Deer Park, Key House and Chain Bridge. *FWS 1730*

Hemington. At least three young ladies can be seen in this *c*.1912 view outside the elegant ivy-clad mansion type house on Ladies Close Hill. The Ferrers and Harpurs were once resident in the old Hemington Hall. *FWS 626*

Hemington. Many old beamed and thatched houses existed *c*.1912 in Hemington in the parish of Lockington. The stream on the right is not so large today. *FWS 627*

Hemington. Yet again Scarratt has captured four more young ladies *c.*1913 about to pass through the stile off Ladies Close Hill. *FWS 785*

Kegworth. Looking down Derby Road *c.*1912. The Temperance Hall and Kegworth Motor Cycle works are clearly in view on the near right-hand side. *FWS 628*

Kegworth. Three small boys have obliged FWS for this *c.*1914 view of Loughborough Road, Kegworth. Today Kegworth is on the flight path into East Midlands International Airport. *FWS 916*

Kegworth. This is a 1914 photograph looking up the High Street, Kegworth towards St Andrew's Church in the distance. The thatched premises on the right appears to be a small shop with the name Shepherds set in tiles below the window. *FWS 957*

King's Mills. Many young children are sitting down adjacent to the ornate old wooden boathouse at King's Mills, *c.*1911. The ornate wooden building with its wooden verandah was often referred to as the Fishing Lodge. *FWS 472*

King's Mills. The famous chain bridge near Ferry Road, King's Mills. As one drives from Castle Donington to the Priest House today, a form of chain bridge is still evident. This card is unnumbered.

King's Mills. Scarratt's old Morris car in this late 1920s view, parked close to the old cottages at King's Mills with their intricate lattice work wooden porches. *FWS 1345*

King's Mills. The magnificent four-storey gothic style building is today the Priest House hotel and restaurant. It was once part of the Donington Hall estate and was built by William Wilkins in the late eighteenth century. It was partially destroyed by fire and restored as part of the present hotel. This view is *c.*1931. *FWS 1504*

Moira. A superb photograph of Moira and Donisthorpe Institute in 1913 with Scarratt's trusty Douglas motor bike in clear view. The Institute was owned by Moira Colliery Company and was open for only a short while. *FWS 807*

Moira. Scarratt's motor bike is parked on the adjacent platform in this 1913 photograph of Moira Station. *FWS 812*

Moira. A early 1940s production after Scarratt had retired. It is unnumbered

Quorn. Quorn Hall on the bank of the River Soar in 1909. Quorn was at one time referred to as Quorndon. *FWS 297*

Quorn. A 1909 view looking down Leicester Road, Quorn. *FWS 301*

Nottinghamshire

Huthwaite. This pleasing *c.*1911 Scarratt photograph shows Sutton Road and the corner of Carnarvon Grove with four white-smocked youngsters in view. The shop on the right-hand corner is the butcher's premises of B.Shore. *FWS 443*

Sutton Bonnington. A charming scene involving five children playing outside St Michael's Church, Sutton Bonnington, in 1910. The church is of the Early English style, Decorated and Perpendicular periods. *FWS 366*

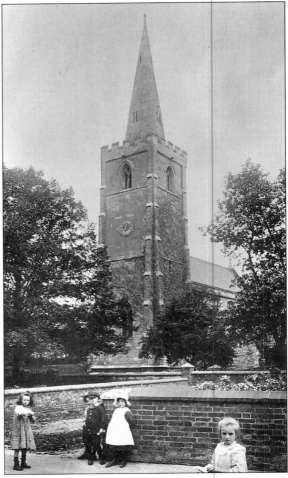

Kingston. This is a late 1920s view of Kingston Hall which was the seat of Lord Belper. It was a brick mansion resembling a Norman chateau. It occupies the site of the residence of the Babbingtons. *FWS 1380*

Staffordshire

Alstonefield. This is the interior of St Peter's Church *c.*1937-38. It is late perpendicular with some Norman remains. It was restored 1875-76. The pulpit and reading desk are of finely carved oak, bearing the date 1637. *FWS 1818*

Alrewas. A *c.*1911 view from the churchyard of the lych-gates of All Saints' Church. *FWS 551*

Alrewas. A fine close-up of Scarratt's Bullnose Morris open-top motor vehicle NU 7074, situated opposite the thatched house on Park Road, Alrewas *c.*1928. Scarratt's dog, Toby, now starts to appear on the scene. *FWS 1375*

Alrewas. The church of All Saints' shown here *c.*1930, founded 820, partially restored 1854 and 1877, was of the Decorated and Perpendicular style. *FWS 1469*

Alrewas. A late *c*.1930 view looking down Main Street, Alrewas. FWS's faithful dog Toby and minder are in the picture once more. *FWS 1471*

Alrewas. That dog again, this time at The Square, Alrewas, *c*.1930. This view looking towards the canal bridge. *FWS 1473*

Burton upon Trent. This is an early 1907 blue print of the Outwoods Recreation Ground situated on the west side of Burton upon Trent. The ground was landscaped *c.*1880. *FWS 112*

Burton upon Trent. This is a fine 1908 illustration of the ornate iron Ferry Bridge at Stapenhill, built by Thornewill & Wareham in 1889. *FWS 221*

Burton upon Trent. There were many fine walks along the river in Burton upon Trent. This view is *c*.1909. *FWS 262*

Burton upon Trent. Scarratt's cycle is carefully placed against the fifteenth-century wall of the gateway to the former Burton Abbey, shown here *c*.1912. The widening of Lichfield Street demolished all. *FWS 619*

Mayfield. This *c.*1907 view looking towards the ancient stone Hanging Bridge at Mayfield with the River Dove was an unnumbered coloured production.

Mayfield. An early Scarratt brown print showing the cottage (formerly Stancliffe Farm) of Tom Moore, the famous poet and ballad writer in *c.*1907. Locals rest in the field above the river bank in front of Slack Lane. The Irish poet lived here for only a short period around 1815. Thomas Moore wrote most of *Lalla Rookh* whilst in this cottage. One of his children, Olivia, is buried in the churchyard of St John the Baptist. *FWS 108*

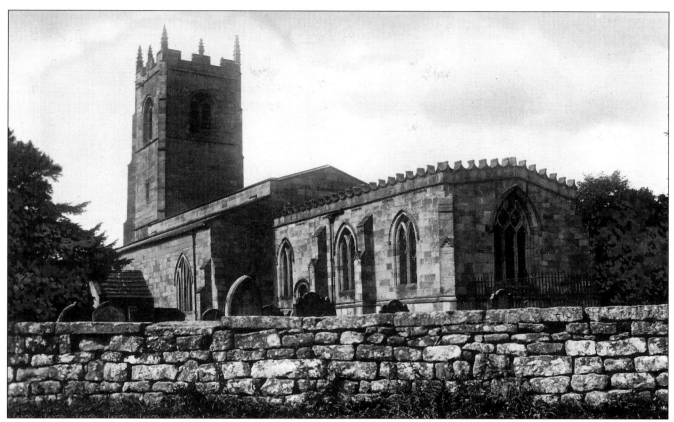

Mayfield. This *c.*1916 view shows the embattled and pinnacled tower of Mayfield's Church of St John the Baptist. There is allegedly a connection with Bonnie Prince Charlie, this being two holes in the church tower door made by musket balls from his retreating troops in 1745. The choir have won many competitions. *FWS 1062*

View towards Tutbury from the Derbyshire side of the Dove. Many children gather outside the Railway Hotel, Hatton, in this *c.*1907 blue print illustration, looking towards Tutbury Station. *FWS 124*

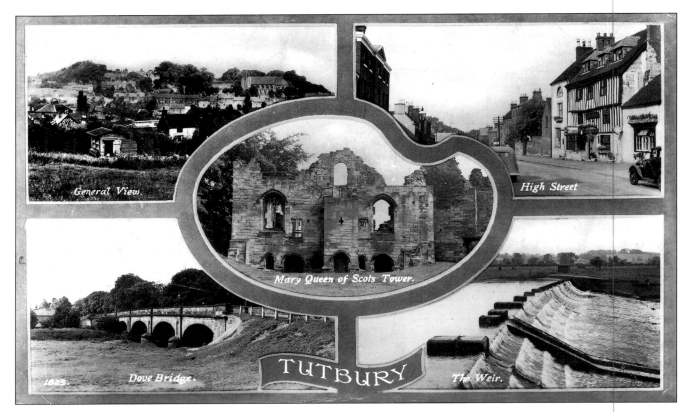

Tutbury. This five panel multi-view is one of the last photographs published by Scarratt & Co during the late 1930s. The famous Dog and Partridge inn can be seen top right. The centre panel shows the ruins of the Mary, Queen of Scots Tower at Tutbury Castle. *FWS 1825*

Tutbury, *c.*1934. This shows the superb stained glass and figures contained within the Memorial Chapel at Tutbury. *FWS 1641*

Barton and Walton Station, situated one mile west of Walton-on-Trent on the Derby, Burton and Birmingham section of the Midland Railway and London & North Western Railway, was at Barton in Staffordshire on the other side of the River Trent. Scarratt's trademark, his motor bike, is parked on the platform by the station *c.*1914 as a steam train approaches the platform. *FWS 875*

Appendix A

Scarratt Types

Over the years Frank Scarratt experimented with the presentation of his photographic images when sold as postcards and the following examples show the types thus far discovered by the author.

Colour type

Scarratt's first publications (numbers 1-201 approximately) were all colour printed abroad, either multi-coloured or in a colour wash (green, brown or blue). A number of early colour illustrations exist without numbers and these were generally produced between 1906 and 1908. This card, issued unnumbered, shows Mary Scarratt in the lane leading to All Saints' Church, Ockbrook. It was in multi-colour.

Colour type with brown border

This type was published infrequently and is found only in a few cards numbered below 200 (*eg* 107 Mill Hill, 186 Shot Tower etc.) Here we see the Infectious Hospital at Little Chester, also known as the Isolation Hospital. Many Derbeians had the dubious pleasure of staying here. The hospital's tall chimney was a well-known landmark on the fringe of Chaddesden. This view was taken *c.*1908. On the reverse of this card we can see Scarratt's monogram which he used on some of his work. *FWS 188*

Oval scroll type

This view of St Clement's Church, Horsley,

was printed within an elaborate scroll. It is multi-coloured and was published *c.*1908. *FWS 199*.

Photographic type with white border

Scarratt produced several batches of black and white and sepia photographic illustrations with a plain white border. The main batches were found in numbers 200-233 (*c.*1908) and numbers 889-1846 (*c.*1914-1938). This one shows Scarratt's motor bike and his travelling companion from the firm of Wildt & Kray in Derby Road, Hulland Ward, in the mid 1920s. *FWS 1250*

Photographic type without border

Scarratt produced many photographic illustrations like the one above, usually in black and white or sepia tone. They are generally found in numbers above 889 (*c.*1914-1938) but several earlier publications have been noted. This one shows Scarratt's daughter (in straw boater) outside the public baths in Full Street, Derby, *c.*1912. The original Silk Mill public house is in the distance. *FWS 639*.

Upright view

Some of Scarratt's cards were published in upright form, as this one with an ornate framed border. It shows ladies in their finery taking a stroll down the tree-lined Lovers' Walk at Matlock, *c.*1911. *FWS 511*

Photographic type with ornate fancy border

Scarratt's ornate framed border publications were his 'flagship'. His own artistic talent, coupled with his experience as a wallpaper designer, produced many different styles as shown below:

The Black House, Quarndon.

CHURCH STREET, OCKBROOK.

CHAPEL STREET, SPONDON.

VICTORIA ROAD, DRAYCOTT.

Ferry Bridge Stapenhill, Burton.

TOWN HALL, DERBY. FREE LIBRARY.

MARKET STREET, HEANOR.

THE LODGE, KILBURN.

OCKBROOK CHURCH.

CORN MARKET, DERBY.

LITTLEOVER HOLLOW.

ST. JOSEPH'S CHURCH, DERBY.

EGGINGTON ROAD, ETWALL.

Dating F.W. Scarratt's Photographs

It has been possible to date many of Scarratt's publications fairly accurately. One cannot, of course, rely entirely on dating by his own numbering system or by using the postmark date. However, if the following 'benchmark' dates are taken into account, coupled with his system, then dating becomes much more accurate.

1. Scarratt and family moved to 114 Abbey Street, Derby, in 1906.
2. Scarratt's first postcard published in 1906.
3. Postcard number 100 (Chellaston) sent to Germany for printing in 1906.
4. Several postcards posted in 1906 (*eg*

numbers 79, 96, 97).

5. All postcards up to 383 published from Abbey Street.

6. Scarratt moved to 115 Normanton Road, Derby, in 1910.

7. Postcard number 97 is of Queen Victoria's statue which was unveiled on The Spot, Derby, in 1906; the card is also postmarked 1906 so it cannot be later.

8. Postcard number 207 (Rowditch, Derby) must be dated shortly after the tramlines were laid in 1907.

9. Postcard number 224 (Draycott) shows Jardine's Lace Mill which was opened in 1907; the card is postmarked 1908.

10. Postcard number 349 (Belper) must be dated shortly after Herbert Strutt's School was opened in 1909.

11. Postcard number 360 (Normanton Recreation Ground) must be dated shortly after the ground was opened in 1909.

12. Postcard number 363 (Nottingham Road) is dated shortly after the tramlines were laid in 1908.

13. Postcard numbers 427, 437, 443, 478, 491, 496, 500 & 558 are all postmarked 1911 and so cannot be later.

14. Postcard number 650 (Aston upon Trent) is postmarked 1912 so the publication can be no later.

15. Postcard number 712 (Kilburn) must be shortly after the Mission Room was opened in 1912.

16. Postcard number 726 must be shortly after the Technical School was completed in 1912.

17. Postcard number 760 (London Road) must be shortly after the new bank building was completed in 1912.

18. Postcard number 836 (Spondon) is postmarked 1914 and so can be no later.

19. Postcard number 867 (Derby Arboretum) is postmarked January 1914 and so must be c.1914.

20. Postcard number 895 (Free Library, The Wardwick) must be shortly prior to the extensions to that building in 1915).

21. Postcard numbers 908 & 909 were sent to Rotary for printing in 1914.

22. Postcard numbers 943-945 (Breadsall) were after the 1914 fire and prior to the restoration which was completed in 1916.

23. Postcard numbers 976 & 977 (Derby Hippodrome) must be after the theatre opened in 1913.

24. Postcard numbers 1020 & 1021 (Castle Donington Hall) show sentry box and wire; the hall was used as a prisoner-of-war camp during World War One.

25. Postcard number 1056 (Littleover Hollow) is postmarked 1916 and so can be no later.

26. Postcard number 146 (Chain Lane) sent to Wildt & Kray for printing in 1924.

27. Postcard number 1181 (Derby War Memorial) must be before 1925 as Barlow & Taylor premises not yet built.

28. Postcard numbers 1258, 1260 & 1261 (Alvaston Lake) must be after the lake was opened in 1923.

29. Postcard number 1308 (Derby War Memorial) must either after unveiling in 1924 or after Barlow & Taylors was built in 1925.

30. Postcard number 1415 (Yard Lane, Swarkestone) is postmarked 1931 so cannot be later.

31. Postcard number 1549 (Chellaston) posted in 1932 so cannot be later.

32. Postcard number 1576 (Exeter Bridge) must be after the widening and new bridge in 1931.

33. Postcard number 1587 (Sadler Gate) must be during the floods of 1932.

34. Postcard number numbers 1710 & 1712 (Derby River Gardens) must be after the gardens were opened in 1934; the card is postmarked 1936.

35. Postcard number 1674 was taken during the 1935 Jubilee celebrations.

36. Postcard number 1804 (Coliseum, London Road) must after the building was converted to a cinema in 1934.

37. Scarratt retired in 1938.

Although 33 postcards have so far been found without any identification numbers, Scarratt usually gave each of his publications a unique number (although he occasionally erred and used the same number twice). Numbering of his early coloured and photographic issues was generally on the reverse side of the postcard, whilst later illustrations carried the number on the front. The following is a guide to these dates:

Published from 114 Abbey Street
1-100, 1906
101-258, 1907-1908
259-389, 1908-1910.
Published from 115 Normanton Road
390-500, 1910-1911
501-650, 1911-1912
651-795, 1912-1913
796-950, 1913-1914
951-1056, 1914-1916
Published from Derby Market Hall
1057-1130, 1916-1918
1131-1200, 1918-1924
1201-1340, 1924-1927
1341-1550, 1927-1932
1551-1710, 1932-1936
1711-1846, 1936-1938.

Certain issues do not appear to fit in with the above. For example: number 1010 was previously issued as number 342 published from Normanton Road; numbers 228, 232, 342 & 350 were all published from Normanton Road; numbers 289, 425 & 428 were each published from the Market Hall. It is probable that Scarratt would taken a later photograph and allocate an earlier number, or use up old pre-printed postcard reverse-side paper.

Between numbers 1 & 1846 there are many numbers not allocated. There could be two reasons for this: either Scarratt simply did not use that particular number (which must be so in some cases); or – a much more tantalising prospect for the collector – these are rare postcard publications still out there somewhere, waiting to be discovered.

Appendix B

The following listings forms an index of Francis William Scarratt's lifetime's work. The author would be pleased to hear of of any publications to add to this record. *Denotes a 'benchmark' card.

No	Place	Scene	Print Type	Where Published	Border Type	Date Posted	Prob Date
	Alport		Sepia				
	Barton	Three multi view	B/W				
	Borrowash	Station		Abbey Street	Ornate		1909
	Borrowash	The Cascade (the Waterfall)			Ornate		
	Borrowash	The Bridge					
	Derby	Queen Street (Tram & Church)	Colour			1907	1907
	Derby	Florence Nightingale Statue	Sepia	Normanton Road			1925
	Derby	The Council House	Sepia				1940's
	Derby	Normanton Recreation Ground			Ornate		
	Derby	St Werburgh's Church	Sepia				
	Derby	Christ Church	Sepia (Vert)		Ornate		
	Derby	Entrance to Royal Show June 27-30th 1906	B/W				1906
	Derby	Wardwick and Strand	B/W		Ornate		
	Derby	Green Lane			Ornate		
	Derby	Bradshaw Way	B/W		Deckle		1930
	Derby	Derbyshire Royal Infirmary	B/W		Ornate	1909	1908-09
	Derby	River Gardens	B/W				
	Derby	St Peter's Churchyard		Normanton Road			
	Derby	Markeaton Hall and Gardens	Sepia	Normanton Road			
	Derby	Town hall and Free Library			Ornate		1911
	Elvaston	Castle and Church x 2 ovals		Abbey Street	Ornate	1911	1910
	Etwall	Church Hill and Square	Colour	Abbey Street			1908
	Grindon	Graham Whites Aeroplane 28 April 1910		AV Green			1910
	King's Mills	Chain Bridge	Sepia	Market Hall			
	King's Newton	Gayborder Nurseries, Main Street	B/W				1938
	Mayfield	Hanging Bridge	Colour				1907
	Mickleover	Market Place	Colour	Abbey Street		1907	1906
	Mickleover	Church	Colour	Abbey Street		1906	1906
	Mickleover	Cackle Hill	Colour	Abbey Street		1906	1906
	Ockbrook	Green Lane	Colour	Abbey Street		1907	1906
	Ockbrook	The Settlement	Colour	Abbey Street			1906
	Sutton in Ashfield	Low Street (Heart)	Sepia				
	Wirksworth	St Mary's Church	B/W				1940
17	Belper	River Gardens	Colour	Abbey Street	White		1906
78	Repton	Cross & Church	Green	Normanton Road			1906
79	Derby	St John's Church	Colour	Abbey Street		1906	1906
80	Derby	St Mary's Bridge	Colour	Abbey Street			1906
85	Castle Donington	Castle Donington Hall	Colour	Abbey Street			1906
86	Ashby-de-la-Zouch	Royal Hotel & Tram	Colour	Abbey Street			1906
87	Little Eaton	Church	Colour	Abbey Street		1911	1906
88	Findern	Church	Colour (Vert)	Abbey Street		1911	1906
89	Repton	The Archway	Colour	Abbey Street			1906
90	Weston-on-Trent	Church Gateway	Colour	Abbey Street			1906
91	Ambergate	Station (from the Woods)	Colour	Abbey Street			1906
92	Chaddesden	New Cemetery	Colour	Abbey Street			1906
93	Weston-on-Trent	Cliff view of cows in field	Colour	Abbey Street			1906
94	Little Eaton	The Woods	Colour	Abbey Street			1906
95	Belper	St Peter's Church	Colour	Abbey Street			1906
96	Ashby-de-la-Zouch	Parish Church	Colour	Abbey Street			1906
96	Derby	Kedleston Rd/St Aiden's Church	Colour	Abbey Street		1906	1906
97	Ashby-de-la-Zouch	Bath Street, tram & Post Office	Colour	Abbey Street			1906
97	Derby	Queen Victoria Statue	Colour	Abbey Street		1906	1906*
97	Darley Dale	Whitworth Institute		Abbey Street			1906
98	Derby	Kedleston Road	Colour	Abbey Street			1906
99	Ashby-de-la-Zouch	Burton Road, tram looking down	Colour	Abbey Street			1906
100	Chellaston	Street scene	Colour	Abbey Street		1906	1906
101	Shadlow	Street scene	Colour	Abbey Street			1907
102	Twyford	Anchor Church	Colour (Vert)	Abbey Street			1907
103	Kirk Langley	Church (same as 220)	Blue	Abbey Street		1907	1907
104	Brailsford	Church	Blue	Abbey Street		1908	1907
105	Spondon	The Lodge (same as 216)	Blue	Abbey Street		1908	1907
106	Spondon	Lodge Lane (men on bikes)	Blue	Abbey Street		1908	1907
107	Spondon	St Werburgh's Church	Blue	Abbey Street	Brown		1907
107	Derby	Mill Hill	Colour	Abbey Street	Brown		1907
108	Mayfield	Poet Tom Moore's cottage	Blue	Abbey Street			1907

No	Place	Scene	Print Type	Where Published	Border Type	Date Posted	Prob Date
109	Mayfield	Bridge	Blue	Abbey Street			1907
111	Burton upon Trent	Bridge from Trent	Sepia	Abbey Street			1907
112	Burton upon Trent	Outwoods Recreation Grounds	Blue	Abbey Street		1908	1907
113	Newton Solney	Church	Blue	Abbey Street			1907
114	Barton under Needwood	The Canal	Brown	Abbey Street			1907
115	Barton under Needwood	Church	Brown	Abbey Street			1907
116	Lichfield	Borrow Cop House	Green	Abbey Street			1907
117	Rolleston-on-Dove	Church and river	Colours	Abbey Street		1908	1907
118	Rolleston-on-Dove	Tutbury Road	Green	Abbey Street			1907
119	Rolleston-on-Dove	Armshouse	Colour	Abbey Street		1920	1907
120	Repton	Cross & Church	Colour	Abbey Street			1907
121	Barton under Needwood	Main Street	Colour	Abbey Street		1909	1907
122	Alrewas	Main Street	Colour	Abbey Street			1907
123	Alrewas	The Green & Post Office	Colour	Abbey Street			1907
124	Tutbury	Hatton & Tutbury Station (street scene)	Blue	Abbey Street		1908	1907
125	Mickleover	Hollow	Blue	Abbey Street			1907
126	Castle Donington	Old Farm House (Key House)	Colours	Abbey Street			1907
127	Coxbench	Street scene (Horsley Lane)	Green	Abbey Street			1907
128	Borrowash	Victoria Avenue (cyclists)	Blue	Abbey Street		1910	1907
129	Crich	Street scene	Colour	Abbey Street			1907
130	Whatstandwell	Street scene	Blue	Abbey Street			1907
132	Derby	Brook Walk	Colour	Abbey Street	White	1909	1907
133	Derby	Cowley Street, from Recreation Ground	Colour	Abbey Street	White	1908	1907
134	Littleover	Old Cottage, Littleover Lane	Colour	Abbey Street	White		1907
135	Hilton	The Bridges	Colour	Abbey Street	White		1907
136	King's Mills	King's Mills Lane, chain bridge	Blue (Vert)	Abbey Street	White		1907
137	King's Mills	King's Mills Lane, chain bridge	Colour	Abbey Street	White		1907
138	Borrowash	Derby Road	Colour	Abbey Street		1909	1907
140	Mayfield	Church	Colour	Abbey Street	White		1907
141	Little Eaton	The Hermit (Alice)	Green	Abbey Street			1907
142	Draycott	Station Road	Brown	Abbey Street			1907
143	Derby	Duffield Road, Five Lamps	Colour	Abbey Street			1907
144	Derby	Uttoxeter New Road, tram	Colour	Abbey Street	White		1907
145	Derby	Friar Gate, tram	Colour	Abbey Street	White		1907
146	Derby	Bridge and tram, Nottingham Road	Colour	Abbey Street	White		1907
147	Allestree	Smithy and street scene	Colour	Abbey Street			1907
148	Derby	Kedleston Road, tram and cart	Colour	Abbey Street	Green	1909	1907
149	Quarndon	Quarndon	Green(Vert)	Abbey Street			1907
150	Stapenhill	Bandstand	Green	Abbey Street	White		1907
151	Stapenhill	Cherry Orchard	Blue/green	Abbey Street	White		1907
152	Stapenhill	Recreation	Green(Vert)	Abbey Street			1907
153	Stapenhill	Ferry Bridge	Colour	Abbey Street			1908
154	Mayfield	Yew Tree Lane	Colour	Abbey Street			1908
155	Stapenhill	Ferry Bridge	Blue/green	Abbey Street			1908
155	Mayfield	Old Yew Tree (lane)	Green	Abbey Street			1908
155	Barton under Needwood	Main Street, looking west	Colour	Abbey Street			1908
156	Mayfield	Leek Road	Colour	Abbey Street			1908
157	Lichfield	Pipe Green Woods	Blue	Abbey Street	White		1908
158	Shardlow	Cavendish Bridge	GrP&B/P&BrP	Abbey Street			1908
159	Weston-on-Trent	Village scene	Colour	Abbey Street			1908
160	Newton Solney	Village	Colour	Abbey Street			1908
161	Newton Solney	Trent Lane	Brown/blue	Abbey Street			1908
162	Burton upon Trent	Newton Road	Colour	Abbey Street	White		1908
163	Burton upon Trent	Outwards Recreation Grounds	Blue & sepia	Abbey Street			1908
164	Barton under Needwood	Main Street, east	Colour	Abbey Street		1909	1908
165	Barton under Needwood	Main Street, west	Colour	Abbey Street		1909	1908
166	Barton under Needwood	Tunstall Road	Colour	Abbey Street	White		1908
167	Burton upon Trent	Newton Road	Colour	Abbey Street	White		1908
168	Belper	River Gardens/bandstand	GrP&BrP	Abbey Street			1908
169	Belper	River Gardens/tea rooms	Blue	Abbey Street			1908
170	Belper	River Gardens	Green	Abbey Street			1908
173	Belper	Bandstand	Colour	Abbey Street			1908
175	Kings Bromley	Church	Colour	Abbey Street			1908
176	Walton-on-Trent	Scene	GrP&B/P&BrP	Abbey Street			1908
177	Hatton	Street scene	Brown	Abbey Street		1908	1908
178	Willington	Railway bridge and cart	Blue	Abbey Street		1910	1908
179	Repton	Burton Road	Colour	Abbey Street	White		1908
180	Idridgehay	Church	Colour	Abbey Street	White		1908
181	Hazlewood	Wooden Lane	Blue	Abbey Street			1908
182	Horsley	Church and fountain (same as 711)	Green	Abbey Street		1908	1908
183	Coxbench	Mrs Gray's cottage	Green	Abbey Street			1908

No	Place	Scene	Print Type	Where Published	Border Type	Date Posted	Prob Date
184	Kilburn	Bywell Lane	Blue	Abbey Street			1908
185	Derby	Arboretum, Entrance House	Colour	Abbey Street	White		1908
186	Derby	Shot Tower	Colour(Vert)	Abbey Street	Brown		1908
188	Little Chester	Infectious Hospital	Colour	Abbey Street	Brown		1908
189	Rolleston-on-Dove	Burton Road	Colour	Abbey Street	Brown		1908
190	Rolleston-on-Dove	Hall	Colour	Abbey Street	Brown		1908
191	Littleover	The Hollow	Colour	Abbey Street	Ornate		1908
192	Dovedale	Peveril in the Peak Hotel	Green	Abbey Street			1908
192	Chaddesden	New Cemetery	Colour	Abbey Street			1908
193	Milford	Tunnel	GrP	Abbey Street			1908
194	Mayfield	Five-pallet multi view	Colour	Abbey Street	Pallete		1908
195	Burton upon Trent	Trent Bridge	Colour	Abbey Street	Scrowel		1908
196	Burton upon Trent	Outwoods Recreation Grounds	Colour	Abbey Street	Scrowel		1908
197	Rolleston-on-Dove	Hall	Colour	Abbey Street	Scrowel		1908
198	Coxbench	Coxbench, near Derby	Colour Oval	Abbey Street	Scrowel		1908
199	Horsley	Horsley Church, near Derby		Abbey Street	Scrowel		1908
200	Borrowash	Derby Road, pub and animation	Colour	Abbey Street	Scrowel		1908
200	Two Dales	Street scene		Abbey Street			1908
201	Burton upon Trent	Humorous	Colour	Abbey Street			1908
204	Derby	Great Northern Bridge, Friar Gate		Abbey Street		1910	1908
205	Derby	Becket Street, coach and horses	B/W	Abbey Street		1912	1908
206	Derby	Kedleston Road, tram	B/W	Abbey Street		1909	1908
207	Derby	Uttoxeter Old and New Road, tram	B/W	Abbey Street			1908*
208	Derby	Gerald Street School, milk cart	B/W (Vert)	Abbey Street			1908
209	Ockbrook	Lecture Hall, street scene	B/W	Abbey Street	White	1908	1908
210	Ockbrook	Flood Street, cart and pub	B/W	Abbey Street			1908
211	Mackworth	Castle gateway	B/W	Abbey Street	White	1909	1908
212	Barton under Needwood	Upper Main Street	B/W	Abbey Street			1908
213	Barton under Needwood	Vicarage and cart	B/W	Abbey Street			1908
216	Spondon	The Lodge (same as 105)		Abbey Street	Ornate		1908
218	Holbrook	Church Street		Abbey Street			1908
220	Kirk Langley	Church (same as 103)		Abbey Street	Ornate		1908
221	Burton upon Trent	Ferry Bridge	Colour	Abbey Street			1908
222	Burton upon Trent	Belvedere Road		Abbey Street	Ornate		1908
223	Little Eaton	View from bridge	B/W	Abbey Street	White		1908
224	Draycott	Jardine Lace Mill	B/W (Vert)	Abbey Street			1908*
225	Etwall	Street scene		Abbey Street	Ornate	1909	1908
226	Etwall	Blacksmith's Hill	B/W	Abbey Street			1908
227	Marston-on-Dove	Church		Abbey Street	White		1908
228	Chaddesden	Church	B/W	Normanton Road			1908
229	Yoxall	Church					1908
230	Yoxall	The Green, horse and cart, workman	Sepia	Abbey Street	White		1908
231	Quarndon	Church	B/W (Vert)	Abbey Street			1908
232	Allestree	Church	B/W	Normanton Road			1908
233	Allestree	The Poplars	B/W	Abbey Street	White		1908
234	Polesworth	Church and Vicarage					1908
236	Polesworth	The Square		Abbey Street			1908
237	Polesworth	Bridge Street	Colour	Abbey Street	Oval		1908
238	Derby	Wardwick and Strand, tram		Abbey Street	Ornate		1908
239	Derby	Derbyshire Royal Infirmary		Abbey Street	Ornate		1908
240	Derby	Green Lane, children		Abbey Street	Ornate		1908
243	Derby	Duffield Road, car, Mile Ash		Abbey Street	Ornate		1908
246	Barton under Needwood	Church (same as 115)	Brown	Abbey Street			1907
248	Derby	Union Workhouse, gates		Abbey Street	Ornate	1910	1908
249	Derby	Friar Gate, tram		Abbey Street	Ornate		1908
250	Ockbrook	The Settlement, view of houses (same as 757)		Abbey Street	Ornate	1910	1908
252	Ockbrook	The Settlement, houses		Abbey Street	Ornate	1910	1908
253	Ockbrook	Green Lane		Abbey Street	Ornate	1910	1908
254	Melbourne	Pool and church		Abbey Street	Oval		1908
255	Hanbury	Church Lane		Abbey Street	Oval		1908
256	Hanbury	Church		Abbey Street	Ornate	1910	1908
257	Hanbury	Village pump, street scene and church		Abbey Street	Ornate		1908
258	Hanbury	Martins Lane	(Vert)	Abbey Street	Ornate	1908	1908
260	Derby	Three-panel multi view (centre circle)		Abbey Street			1908
261	Barton under Needwood	Multi view	(Vert)	Abbey Street			1909
262	Stapenhill	River Gardens		Abbey Street	Ornate		1909
263	Stapenhill	Recreation shelter		Abbey Street	Ornate		1909
264	Burton upon Trent	Bass barrels	B/W	Abbey Street			1909
265	Burton upon Trent	St Paul's Church		Abbey Street			1909
267	Stapenhill	Recreation grounds	Sepia	Abbey Street	Oval		1909
268	Repton	Cross and church		Abbey Street			1909

No	Place	Scene	Print Type	Where Published	Border Type	Date Posted	Prob Date
269	Repton	Cross and church		Abbey Street	Oval		1909
271	Alrewas	The Green	Sepia	Abbey Street	Ornate		1909
275	Belper	Clock tower and street		Abbey Street	Ornate	1914	1909
276	Belper	Market Place	Sepia	Abbey Street	Ornate		1909
277	Belper	Bridge Street, animation		Abbey Street	Ornate		1909
278	Derby	Uttoxeter New Road, tram		Abbey Street	Ornate		1909
279	Derby	Two oval multi, Hall/Library	B/W	Abbey Street			1909
280	Elvaston	Two oval multi, Church/Castle	B/W	Abbey Street			1909
281	Little Eaton	Multi view x two oval		Abbey Street			1909
282	Spondon	Two views, Lodge and lane	(Vert)	Abbey Street	Ornate		1909
284	Derby	St Werburgh's Church	(Vert)	Abbey Street	Oval		1909
285	Quorn	Wood Lane		Abbey Street	Oval & ornate		1909
287	Quorn	Church		Abbey Street	Ornate		1909
288	Aston-on-Trent	The Lodge		Abbey Street	Oval		1909
289	Aston-on-Trent	Church and cart		Market Hall	Oval	1915	1909
292	Weston-on-Trent	Weston Cliff		Abbey Street	Oval		1909
293	Weston-on-Trent	Canal bridge		Abbey Street	Oval		1909
294	Quorn	Quorn Hall from lawn (man at side)		Abbey Street	Ornate		1909
296	Quorn	Quorn Hall from lawn		Abbey Street	Ornate		1909
297	Quorn	Quorn Hall from river		Abbey Street	Ornate		1909
298	Quorn	Bridge and river		C.Gamble	Ornate		1909
300	Quorn	Quorn village		C.Gamble	Ornate		1909
301	Quorn	Leicester Road, houses on right		Abbey Street	Ornate		1909
302	Quorn	Cross Brook		Abbey Street	Ornate		1909
305	Burton upon Trent	Bearwood Hill, looking up		Abbey Street	Ornate		1909
306	Burton upon Trent	Trent Bridge	B/W	Abbey Street			1909
307	Burton upon Trent	Station Road, large tram		Abbey Street	Ornate		1909
308	Burton upon Trent	High Street, tram (same as 593)	Colour	Abbey Street	Ornate		1909
309	Burton upon Trent	Market Place		Abbey Street	Ornate		1909
310	Matlock	High Tor		Abbey Street	Ornate	1911	1909
312	Two Dales	Brookside		Abbey Street	Ornate	1911	1910
314	Barrow upon Soar	The Bridge	Square	Abbey Street	Ornate		1910
316	Kilburn	Chapel Street		Abbey Street	Ornate		1910
317	Kilburn	Church Street		Abbey Street	Ornate	1913	1910
318	Horsley Woodhouse	School		Abbey Street	Ornate		1910
319	Horsley Woodhouse	Church and vicarage		Abbey Street	Ornate		1910
320	Hilton	Lodge		Abbey Street	Ornate		1910
321	Hilton	The weir		Abbey Street	Ornate		1910
322	Sutton-on-the-Hill	Street scene, lane houses, horse and girl		Abbey Street	Ornate		1910
323	Quarndon	Black House and road	B/W and Colour	Abbey Street	Ornate	1913	1910
324	Allestree	Street scene		Abbey Street	Oval		1910
325	Derby	Burton Road, trams and terminus		Abbey Street	Ornate	1910	1910
327	Derby	Long Bridge and weir		Abbey Street	Ornate		1910
328	Derby	London Road, tram	B/W	Abbey Street	Ornate	1912	1910
329	Derby	Midland Station, two trams		Abbey Street	Ornate		1910
330	Derby	St John's Church		Abbey Street	Ornate		1910
331	Derby	Kedleston Road from Five Lamps		Abbey Street		1910	1910
332	Derby	Corn Market, horse, carts and trams		Abbey Street	Ornate		1910
333	Derby	Albert Street (Palace)		Abbey Street	Ornate		1910
334	Derby	St Andrew's Church	(Vert)	Abbey Street	Ornate	1911	1910
336	Derby	Markeaton Recreation, paddling		Abbey Street	Ornate	1912	1910
337	Derby	Markeaton Recreation, paddling		Abbey Street	Ornate	1911	1910
338	Derby	Burton Road, from Carmel Mount, tram		Abbey Street	Ornate	1910	1910
339	Littleover	Entrance to Littleover		Abbey Street	Ornate	1910	1910
340	Milford	Church		Abbey Street	Ornate		1910
341	Shardlow	Street scene		Abbey Street	Ornate		1910
342	Milford	Bridge and weirs from the rock (same as 1010)		Normanton Road		1913	1910
343	Milford	Hopping Hill and church		Abbey Street	Ornate		1910
345	Quarndon	Bunkers Hill, near Derby, tree on hill		Abbey Street	Ornate		1910
346	Quarndon	Jacobson's House		Abbey Street	Ornate	1911	1910
347	Allestree	Street scene		Abbey Street	Oval		1910
348	Duffield	Church		Abbey Street			1910
349	Belper	Herbert Strutt Higher School		Abbey Street	Ornate	1917	1910*
350	Holbrook	Convalescent Home		Normanton Road	Oval	1913	1910
351	Holbrook	Convalescent Home		Normanton Road	Ornate		1910
353	Ednaston	The Lodge, garden		Abbey Street	Ornate		1910
358	Derby	Osmaston Hall	Sepia	Abbey Street	Ornate	1911	1910
359	Derby	Osmaston Church		Abbey Street	Ornate		1910
360	Derby	Normanton Recreation Ground		Abbey Street	Ornate		1910*
361	Derby	The Arboretum, fountain and children		Abbey Street	Oval		1910
362	Derby	Osmaston Road, tram		Abbey Street	Ornate	1911	1910

No	Place	Scene	Print Type	Where Published	Border Type	Date Posted	Prob Date
363	Derby	Nottingham Road, Cemetery Hill	B/W	Abbey Street	Ornate		1910*
364	Sutton Bonnington	Main Street and post office		Abbey Street	Ornate		1910
365	Sutton Bonnington	Main Street		Abbey Street	Ornate		1910
366	Sutton Bonnington	St Michael's Church	(Vert)	Abbey Street	Ornate		1910
367	Sutton Bonnington	St Anne's Church		Abbey Street	Ornate		1910
369	Shelton Lock	Locks		Abbey Street	Pallete		1910
370	Littleover	The Hollow, cottage	Colour	Abbey Street	Ornate		1910
371	Littleover	The Hollow (Scarratt Brothers)		Abbey Street	Oval		1910
372	Burton upon Trent	Cemetery gates		Abbey Street			1910
373	Littleover	The Hollow, heart, birthday flowers	B/W	Abbey Street			1910
373	Stapenhill	Church	(Vert)	Abbey Street	Ornate		1910
374	Burton upon Trent	Water tower		Abbey Street	Pallete		1910
376	Barrow upon Trent	The Lodge		Abbey Street	Pallete		1910
377	Barrow upon Trent	Church	Sepia	Abbey Street	Ornate		1910
378	Coxbench	Coxbench station, exterior		Abbey Street	Ornate		1910
379	Little Eaton	Entrance to quarries	Sepia	Abbey Street	Pallete	1912	1910
380	Derby	Five multi view	Sepia	Abbey Street	Pallete	1911	1910
381	Burton upon Trent	Five multi view		Abbey Street	Pallete		1910
383	Stapenhill	River	Colour	Abbey Street	Ornate		1910
388	Quorn	Quorn House	Sepia	C.Gamble			1910
389	Quorn	River Soar and bridge	Sepia	C.Gamble			1910
390	Quorn	Warner's cottages and Soar Road		C.Gamble	Ornate		1910
392	Alton	Multi view		Normanton Road			1910
393	Alton	Two multi view	Sepia	Normanton Road			1910
394	Alton	Castle		Normanton Road			1910
395	Alton	Church		Normanton Road			1910
396	Alton	Castle		Normanton Road	Ornate		1910
397	Alton	Castle		Normanton Road			1910
398	Alton	Shop and street		Normanton Road	Ornate		1910
399	Littleover	The Hollow, cart and men	(Vert)	Normanton Road	Ornate		1910
400	Quarndon	The Village		Normanton Road	Oval		1910
401	Quarndon	Quarndon Lane, view		Normanton Road	Ornate	1912	1910
402	Darley Abbey	Church and weir	Sepia	Normanton Road	Ornate		1911
403	Darley Abbey	The weir					1911
404	Derby	Entrance to Markeaton		Normanton Road	Ornate		1911
406	Markeaton	Markeaton Brook		Normanton Road	Ornate		1911
408	Derby	St Mary's Church	(Vert)	Normanton Road	Ornate	1912	1911
409	Derby	St Joseph's Church		Normanton Road	Ornate	1912	1911
410	Derby	Burton Road		Normanton Road	Ornate		1911
411	Derby	Burton Road, houses and tram		Normanton Road	Ornate		1911
412	Dunstall	Dunstall Hall, side view		Normanton Road	Pallete		1911
413	Dunstall	Dunstall Church		Normanton Road	Ornate		1911
416	Barton under Needwood	Efflinch, street scene		Normanton Road	Ornate		1911
417	Barton under Needwood	Main street	B/W	Normanton Road	Ornate		1911
418	Barton under Needwood	Dunstall Road		Normanton Road	Ornate		1911
419	Barton under Needwood	The Square		Normanton Road	Ornate		1911
420	Etwall	Street scene		Normanton Road	Oval		1911
421	Etwall	Post office		Normanton Road	Ornate		1911
422	Etwall	Egginton Road		Normanton Road	Ornate		1911
423	Hilton	The Lodge, woman and Scarratt's bicycle		Normanton Road	Pallete		1911
425	Derby	Kedleston Road		Market Hall	Ornate	1920	1911
426	Derby	Rolls-Royce		Normanton Road	Ornate		1911
427	Derby	Rolls-Royce Institute		Normanton Road	Pallete	1911	1911
428	Derby	Old Normanton Church		Market Hall	Pallete	1926	1911
429	Derby	Cavendish Hotel, tram, children, pram		Normanton Road	Pallete		1911
430	Burton upon Trent	Ashby Road		Normanton Road			1911
431	Burton upon Trent	Burton Station exterior, tram		Normanton Road	Ornate		1911
432	Burton upon Trent	King Edward's Place		Normanton Road	Ornate		1911
433	Burton upon Trent	Monument Place		Normanton Road	Pallete		1911
434	Little Eaton	Entrance to	Sepia	Normanton Road	Ornate		1911
435	Darley Abbey	Boating Lake	Sepia	Normanton Road	Pallete		1911
436	Swadlincote	High Street (Salts shop)		Normanton Road	Ornate		1911
437	Swadlincote	Church Street		Normanton Road	Ornate	1911	1911
438	Bretby	Philosopher's Walk		Normanton Road	Pallete		1911
439	Hartshorne	Hudson Old Mill (Lane)		Normanton Road	Pallete		1911
440	Swadlincote	Wragg's Pipe Works		Normanton Road			1911
441	Swadlincote	Hall's Collieries		Normanton Road	Ornate	1912	1911
442	Huthwaite	Main Street		Normanton Road	Ornate		1911
443	Huthwaite	Sutton Road and tram		Normanton Road	Pallete	1911	1911
444	Huthwaite	Sutton Road, terminus and tram		Normanton Road	Ornate		1911
445	Huthwaite	Harper Lane		Normanton Road	Ornate		1911

No	Place	Scene	Print Type	Where Published	Border Type	Date Posted	Prob Date
446	Burton upon Trent	New Street looking towards Abbey		Normanton Road	Ornate		1911
447	Burton upon Trent	Christ Church	(Vert)	Normanton Road	Ornate		1911
452	Darley Dale	Church		Normanton Road	Ornate		1911
453	Darley Dale	Church		Normanton Road	Ornate		1911
454	Mancetter	Church		Normanton Road	Ornate		1911
456	Hartshill(Warwickshire)	The Abbey	Sepia	Normanton Road			1911
457	Hartshill	The Quarry	Sepia	Normanton Road			1911
458	Hartshill	The Green		Normanton Road	Ornate		1911
459	Hartshill	Post Office, Main Road	Sepia	Normanton Road	Ornate		1911
463	Ashbourne	Parish Church		Normanton Road	Oval		1911
464	Ashbourne	Church Street		Normanton Road	Ornate		1911
465	Derby	Normanton Recreation Grounds		Normanton Road			1911
466	Derby	Normanton Recreation Grounds (swings)		Normanton Road	Ornate		1911
467	Derby	Normanton Recreation Grounds		Normanton Road	Oval	1912	1911
468	Derby	Normanton Recreation Grounds		Normanton Road	Oval	1912	1911
469	Derby	Christ Church	(Vert)	Normanton Road	Oval		1911
470	Derby	Five Lamps, Normanton Road		Normanton Road	Pallete	1912	1911
472	King's Mills	The Boathouse		Normanton Road	Oval	1913	1911
473	King's Mills	The Boathouse		Normanton Road			1911
475	King's Mills	The weir		Normanton Road	Ornate		1911
475	Hartshill	The Green		Normanton Road			1911
476	Weston-on-Trent	Weston Church		Normanton Road	Oval		1911
477	Quarndon	Bunkers Hill		Normanton Road	Oval		1911
478	Little Eaton	View from bridge, horse and cart		Normanton Road	Ornate	1911	1911
479	Quorn	Church	B/W	Normanton Road			1911
480	Kirk Langley	Village crossroads, street scene, horses		Normanton Road	Ornate	1913	1911
481	Kirk Langley	Moor Lane		Normanton Road	Ornate		1911
482	Kirk Langley	Flagshaw Lane, horses and man		Normanton Road	Oval		1911
483	Barrow upon Trent	The Hall	Sepia	Normanton Road	Oval		1911
484	Swadlincote	West Street		Normanton Road	Ornate		1911
485	Swadlincote	High Street, tram, horse on right		Normanton Road	Ornate		1911
486	Swadlincote	Upper fish pond		Normanton Road	Oval		1911
487	Bretby	Bretby Hall and Cedar Tree		Normanton Road	Oval		1911
488	Burton upon Trent	Station Street		Normanton Road	Oval		1911
489	Burton upon Trent	Newton Road, two carts		Normanton Road	Ornate		1911
490	Hartshill	Tee's Granite Quarry	Sepia	Normanton Road	White		1911
491	Hartshill	Adult School		Normanton Road		1911	1911
493	Ockbrook	Grange Cottages	B/W	Normanton Road			1911
494	Ockbrook	Church Street		Normanton Road	Oval		1911
495	Ockbrook	Green Lane, houses and people		Normanton Road	Oval		1911
496	Ockbrook	Bare Lane, barn and children		Normanton Road	Oval	1911	1911
498	Ockbrook	Bishops Walk, The Settlement	(Vert)	Normanton Road	Oval		1911
499	Ockbrook	Church		Normanton Road	Oval	1912	1911
500	Ockbrook	From Carr Hill	B/W	Normanton Road	Ornate	1911	1911
501	Ockbrook	Green Lane, street and children		Normanton Road	Oval		1911
502	Derby	Normanton Road, The Green, tram		Normanton Road	Ornate	1913	1911
504	Derby	All Saints Church, horse and cart	(Vert)	Normanton Road	Ornate	1919	1911
505	Derby	Darley, path and road		Normanton Road	Oval		1911
506	Derby	Town Hall, tram		Normanton Road	Ornate	1913	1911
507	Normanton	Church		Normanton Road	Ornate		1911
508	Matlock Bath	Lovers Walk/Ferry		Normanton Road	Oval		1911
509	Matlock Bath	Derwent Parade		Normanton Road		1914	1911
510	Matlock Bath	Tunnel and weir	(Vert)	Normanton Road	Ornate		1911
511	Matlock Bath	Lovers Walk	B/W	Normanton Road	Ornate	1912	1911
512	Matlock Bath	The Derwent		Normanton Road	Pallete		1911
513	Matlock Bath	Promenade and Jubilee Bridge	Sepia	Normanton Road	Oval		1911
514	Matlock	General view		Normanton Road		1920	1911
517	Chatsworth	Chatsworth Bridge	Sepia	Normanton Road	Ornate		1911
518	Chatsworth	Chatsworth House		Normanton Road	Pallete		1911
519	Chatsworth	Chatsworth House		Normanton Road	Ornate	1912	1911
520	Haddon	Haddon Hall	Sepia	Normanton Road	Oval		1911
521	Rowsley	The Peacock		Normanton Road	Ornate	1912	1911
522	Beeley	Chapel Street		Normanton Road	Ornate	1914	1911
523	Beeley	Brook Side and lane		Normanton Road	Oval		1911
524	Beeley	Church		Normanton Road			1911
525	Repton	Church		Normanton Road	Ornate		1911
526	Swadlincote	The Cutting near Swadlincote, tram		Normanton Road	Oval		1911
527	Ashby-de-la-Zouch	Ashby Castle		Normanton Road	Oval		1911
528	Ashby-de-la-Zouch	Ashby Castle from Chapel Side		Normanton Road	Ornate		1911
529	Ashby-de-la-Zouch	Ashby Castle	Sepia (Vert)	Normanton Road	Plain		1911
530	Ashby-de-la-Zouch	Ashby Castle from normal side		Normanton Road	Oval	1912	1911

No	Place	Scene	Print Type	Where Published	Border Type	Date Posted	Prob Date
531	Ashby-de-la-Zouch	Ashby Castle near Chapel		Normanton Road	Pallete		1911
532	Ashby-de-la-Zouch	Manor House		Normanton Road	Pallete		1911
533	Egginton	Egginton		Normanton Road			1911
535	Hilton	Lodge/weir	(Vert)	Normanton Road	Oval		1911
536	King's Mills	The weir/The Boathouse		Normanton Road	x 2 Ovals		1911
538	Long Eaton	Station Street		Normanton Road	Ornate		1911
539	Long Eaton	Main Street		Normanton Road	Ornate	1917	1911
540	Long Eaton	The Green from Market		Normanton Road	Pallete		1911
541	Trent Lock	People boating		Normanton Road	Pallete		1911
542	Derby	Derbyshire Royal Infirmary	Sepia	Normanton Road			1911
543	Trent Lock			Normanton Road	Oval		1911
544	Hartshill	The Windmill (street)		Normanton Road	Ornate		1911
545	Stockingford	Stockingford Colliery		Normanton Road	Ornate		1911
547	Hartshill	Hartshill Church	(Vert)	Normanton Road	Ornate		1911
549	Coxbench	Quarries		Normanton Road			1911
550	Alrewas	Old Cottage	Sepia	Normanton Road	White		1911
551	Alrewas	Lychgates	Sepia	Normanton Road	White		1911
552	Alrewas	All Saints Church		Normanton Road	Pallete		1911
553	Alrewas	Mill Stream		Normanton Road	Ornate		1911
554	Alrewas	Burton Road (Old Royal Oak)		Normanton Road	Ornate		1911
557	Mackworth	Mackworth Castle gateway		Normanton Road	Ornate	1913	1911
558	Mackworth	Mackworth School		Normanton Road		1911	1911*
559	Mackworth	Church		Normanton Road	Pallete		1911
561	Melbourne	House and pool		Normanton Road	Pallete		1911
562	Holbrook	Holbrook Church	Sepia	Normanton Road			1911
563	Holbrook	Coxbench Lane		Normanton Road	Ornate	1912	1911
564	Holbrook	Nether Lea	B/W	Normanton Road	Oval		1911
565	Holbrook	Nether Lea Hall		Normanton Road	Ornate		1911
566	Holbrook	Holbrook (Greyhound pub)	B/W	Normanton Road	Oval		1911
567	Kilburn	The Lodge		Normanton Road	Pallete	1912	1911
568	Breedon-on-the-Hill	The Brook and village		Normanton Road	Pallete		1911
569	Breedon-on-the-Hill	The Green, houses and children		Normanton Road	Ornate		1911
570	Breedon-on-the-Hill	Round House and pub		Normanton Road	Ornate		1911
572	King's Mills	Ferry and House, birthday wishes		Normanton Road			1912
574	Derby	Arboretum, heart, greetings	Sepia	Normanton Road			1912
576	Derby	Arboretum, fountain		Normanton Road	Ornate	1912	1912
577	Derby	Arboretum, aviary		Normanton Road		1914	1912
578	Derby	Arboretum		Normanton Road	Pallete		1912
580	Matlock Bath	Kersall		Normanton Road		1912	1912
581	Quorn	Quorn House, waterfall		C.Gamble	Pallete		1912
583	Little Eaton	From the Quarries		Normanton Road	Ornate		1912
584	Quorn	River Soar and bridge	Sepia	C.Gamble			1912
585	Weston-on-Trent	Street scene		Normanton Road	Ornate		1912
586	Derby	Midland Station	Colour	Normanton Road		1912	1912
588	Derby	Derbyshire Royal Infirmary	Colour	Normanton Road			1912
590	Derby	Albert Street and Palace	Colour	Normanton Road			1912
591	Derby	Becket Street (same as 205)	Colour	Normanton Road		1913	1907/08
592	Derby	Uttoxeter New Road, tram	Colour	Normanton Road			1912
593	Burton upon Trent	High Street, tram	Colour	Normanton Road			1912
594	Burton upon Trent	King Edward's Place	Colour	Normanton Road			1912
595	Burton upon Trent	Market Place	Colour	Normanton Road			1912
596	Darley Dale	Boating Lake	Colour	Normanton Road			1912
597	King's Mills	Boathouse	Colour	Normanton Road			1912
598	Derby	St James's Street		Normanton Road	Ornate		1912
599	Derby	Victoria Street, transport		Normanton Road	Ornate		1912
600	Derby	Metalite Limited, Osmaston Road		Normanton Road	Ornate		1912
601	Derby	Dairyhouse Road, tram		Normanton Road	Ornate	1913	1912
602	Wilne	Wilne Mill		Normanton Road	Ornate		1912
603	Wilne	Church		Normanton Road	Ornate		1912
604	Hilton	Derby and Egginton Road		Normanton Road	Ornate		1912
606	Hilton	Street scene, houses or cottage, feeding hens		Normanton Road	Ornate		1912
608	Hilton	The Mill		Normanton Road	Ornate		1912
609	Melbourne	Market Place		Normanton Road	Ornate		1912
613	Derby	Victoria Street, church	Sepia(Vert)	Normanton Road			1912
614	Derby	Chatsworth Street entrance, Recreation Gnd	Sepia	Normanton Road			1912
617	Wilne	Toll Bridge, house		Normanton Road	Ornate		1912
618	Hilton	Flood Gates		Normanton Road	Ornate		1912
619	Burton upon Trent	Abbey Gate		Normanton Road	Ornate		1912
620	Derby	St Thomas's Street Church		Normanton Road	Ornate		1912
621	Derby	Opera House and Grand Theatre		Normanton Road		1918	1912
622	Castle Donington	High Street	B/W	Normanton Road	Ornate		1912

No	Place	Scene	Print Type	Where Published	Border Type	Date Posted	Prob Date
623	Castle Donington	Market Street		Normanton Road	Ornate		1912
624	Castle Donington	Borough Street	Sepia	Normanton Road	Ornate		1912
626	Hemington	Ladies Close Hill		Normanton Road	Ornate		1912
627	Hemington	Hemington village		Normanton Road	Ornate	1916	1912
628	Kegworth	Derby Road		Normanton Road	Ornate	1913	1912
630	Kegworth	Church Road		Normanton Road			1912
631	Kegworth	Mill Lane and cottages		Normanton Road	Ornate	1913	1912
632	Kegworth	Parish rooms and street		Normanton Road	Ornate		1912
634	Derby	Wardwick	B/W	Normanton Road			1912
635	Derby	Friar Gate (street scene)	Sepia	Market Hall		1911	1912
636	Derby	Ashbourne Road, tram, horse and cart	B/W	Normanton Road		1913	1912
638	Derby	Derwent Street	B/W	Normanton Road		1914	1912
639	Derby	Full Street	Sepia	Market Hall		1923	1912
640	Barton under Needwood	Main Street east (same as 164)		Normanton Road	Ornate		1912
641	Barton under Needwood	Main Street west (same as 165)		Normanton Road	Ornate		1912
643	Burton upon Trent	Three multi view, two bottles, one barrel		Normanton Road			1912
644	Quorn	Wood Lane	B/W	C.Gamble			1912
646	Aston-on-Trent	Post Office		Normanton Road		1913	1912
647	Aston-on-Trent	Weston Road		Normanton Road	Ornate	1917	1912
648	Aston-on-Trent	The Green, street scene and course		Normanton Road	Ornate		1912
650	Aston-on-Trent	Gardens		Normanton Road	Pallette	1912	1912*
651	Weston-on-Trent	Suspension bridge		Normanton Road			1912
652	Draycott	Market Square		Normanton Road	Ornate		1912
653	Draycott	Victoria Road, street scene		Normanton Road	Ornate	1914	1912
654	Draycott	Station Road, Lace Mill		Normanton Road	Pallete	1910	1913
655	Draycott	Derby Road		Normanton Road	Ornate		1913
656	Draycott	Draycott Station		Normanton Road	Ornate		1913
657	Draycott	Station Road, street scene		Normanton Road	Ornate		1913
658	Brailsford	Brailsford Hall	B/W	Normanton Road			1912
659	Hatton	Nestlé Milk Factory, horse dray and workers		Normanton Road	Ornate		1912
660	Quarndon	The Common		Normanton Road	Ornate	1912	1912
661	Quarndon	Old Church	(Vert)	Normanton Road	Oval	1914	1912
664	Derby	Normanton Recreation - 3 views	(Vert)	Normanton Road	Ornate		1912
665	Littleover	Three multi view	(Vert)	Normanton Road	Ornate		1912
666	Derby	Arboretum - three multi view	(Vert)	Market Hall	Ornate	1924	1912
667	Markeaton	Three multi views of brook	(Vert)	Normanton Road			1912
668	Etwall	Etwall Church	B/W	Normanton Road	Ornate		1912
669	Etwall	Almshouses		Normanton Road	Ornate	1913	1912
670	Quorn	High Street	Sepia	C. Gamble			
671	Quorn	Meeting Street	Sepia	C. Gamble			
673	Weston-on-Trent	Suspension Bridge		Normanton Road	Ornate		1912
675	Derby	Kedleston Road School		Normanton Road	Ornate	1913	1912
677	Denby	Smithy House and colliery, street scene		Normanton Road	Ornate	1913	1912
678	Denby	Denby Church	B/W	Normanton Road			1912
679	Denby	Denby Vicarage (Built 1904)	B/W	Normanton Road	Ornate		1912
680	Denby	Denby School		Normanton Road	Ornate		1912
681	Denby	Station	B/W	Normanton Road	Ornate		1912
682	Hulland Ward	Derby Road, pond		Normanton Road	Ornate		1912
683	Hulland Ward	The Green and house	Sepia	Normanton Road	Ornate		1912
684	Hulland Ward	The Vicarage		Normanton Road	Ornate		1912
684	Weston-on-Trent	Little London		Normanton Road			1912
685	Hulland Ward	Church	Sepia	Normanton Road			1912
686	Hulland Ward	Wardgate	Sepia	Normanton Road			1912
689	Derby	Duffield Road, snow scene		Normanton Road	Ornate		1912
690	Markeaton	Lane in snow		Normanton Road	Oval		1912
691	Markeaton		Sepia	Normanton Road	Ornate		1912
694	Barton under Needwood	Wales End		Normanton Road	Ornate		1912
698	Barton under Needwood	Blacksmith's Corner		Normanton Road	Oval		1912
700	Horsley Woodhouse	Sitwell Arms		Normanton Road	Ornate		1912
701	Horsley Woodhouse	Wood Lane		Normanton Road	Pallete		1912
703	Wilne	The Ferry Boat		Normanton Road			1912
705	Blackfordby			Normanton Road			1912
706	Derby	Rosehill Street		Normanton Road		1913	1912
707	Derby	Osmaston Road (tram)		Normanton Road	Ornate		1912
708	Derby	London Road (tram) (same as 1061)		Normanton Road	Ornate		1912
709	Derby	Fountain, Arboretum people		Normanton Road	Ornate		1912
711	Horsley	Horsley Church and fountain (same as 182)		Normanton Road	Ornate		1913
712	Kilburn	Church Street		Normanton Road	Ornate	1913	1913*
713	Kilburn	Church Street		Normanton Road	Ornate	1913	1913*
714	Swadlincote	Tram Depot		Normanton Road	Ornate		1913
715	Swadlincote	Hearthcote Road		Normanton Road	Ornate		1913

No	Place	Scene	Print Type	Where Published	Border Type	Date Posted	Prob Date
716	Swadlincote	Wilmot Road		Normanton Road	Ornate		1913
717	Swadlincote	Midway Road		Normanton Road	Ornate		1913
718	Milford	Bridge and weirs		Normanton Road	Ornate		1913
721	Langley Mill	Station Road		Normanton Road	Ornate		1913
722	Langley Mill	Eastwood Lane (Shop)		Normanton Road	Ornate		1913
723	Langley Mill	Wesleyan Church		Normanton Road	Ornate	1914	1913
724	Heanor	High Street		Normanton Road	Ornate		1913
725	Heanor	Market Street		Normanton Road	Ornate	1913	1913
726	Heanor	Technical School		Normanton Road	Ornate		1913*
727	Heanor	Heanor Church	(Vert)	Normanton Road	Oval		1913
728	Heanor	Mansfield Road		Normanton Road	Ornate	1913	1913
730	Melbourne	Basket and Market Place	Sepia	Normanton Road			1913
731	Melbourne	Pool House		Normanton Road			1913
732	Melbourne	Basket, pool and church	Sepia	Normanton Road			1913
733	Little Eaton	Lighthouse	Sepia	Normanton Road			1913
734	Little Eaton	Quarries, Lighthouse	B/W (Vert)	Normanton Road	Oval		1913
735	Little Eaton	Lighthouse		Normanton Road			1913
736	Swadlincote	Five multi view		Normanton Road	Pallete		1913
737	Quarndon	Five multi view		Normanton Road	Pallete	1913	1913
738	Aston-on-Trent	Five multi view		Normanton Road	Pallete	1916	1913
739	Castle Donington	Five multi view		Normanton Road	Pallete	1914	1913
740	Holbrook	Five multi view		Normanton Road	Pallete		1913
741	Etwall	Five multi view		Normanton Road	Pallete		1913
743	Kirk Langley	Kirk Langley Church		Normanton Road			1913
744	Derby	The Spot	Sepia	Normanton Road			1913
745	Derby	St Peter's Street, tram and horse cart	Sepia	Normanton Road			1913
746	Derby	Kedleston Road, tram and cart	Sepia	Normanton Road			1913
747	Derby	Penny Long Lane	B/W	Normanton Road			1913
748	Darley Dale	Whitworth Institute	Sepia	Normanton Road			1913
750	Darley Dale	In the grounds	Sepia	Normanton Road			1913
751	Darley Dale	The Lake		Normanton Road			1913
754	Sudbury	Sudbury Church	Sepia	Normanton Road			1913
755	Sudbury	The Stocks	Sepia	Normanton Road			1913
757	Ockbrook	Moravian Settlement (same as 250)	Sepia	Normanton Road	White	1919	1908
758	Tutbury	Tutbury Church, west front	B/W	Normanton Road			1913
759	Crich	Street scene	Sepia	Normanton Road			1913
760	Derby	London Road, tram and cart	Sepia	Normanton Road			1913
761	Derby	Osmaston Road	B/W	Normanton Road			1913
762	Derby	Halfpenny Lane	B/W	Normanton Road			1913
763	Etwall	Egginton Road, (2)	B/W	Normanton Road			1913
764	Etwall	Egginton Road, (3)	B/W	Normanton Road			1913
765	Etwall	Egginton Road, (4)	B/W	Normanton Road			1913
766	Etwall	Etwall Church interior	B/W	Normanton Road			1913
767	Woodville	Burton Road (pram)		Normanton Road	Ornate		1913
768	Hartshorne	Nether Hall		Normanton Road	Ornate		1913
769	Midway	(Lower) cottages and street scene		Normanton Road	Ornate		1913
770	Turnditch	Turnditch School		Normanton Road	Ornate		1913
771	Turnditch	Turnditch Church		Normanton Road	Ornate		1913
772	Breaston	Main Street	Sepia	Normanton Road			1913
774	Breaston	Breaston Church	B/W	Normanton Road			1913
775	Breaston	Duck Lane	Sepia	Normanton Road			1913
777	Breaston	Longmoor Lane	B/W	Normanton Road			1913
778	Castle Donington	Convalescent Home	Sepia	Normanton Road			1913
779	Castle Donington	Convalescent Home	Sepia	Normanton Road			1913
780	Castle Donington	Church, interior	Sepia	Normanton Road			1913
781	Castle Donington	Church	Sepia (Vert)	Normanton Road			1913
782	Castle Donington	Castle Donington Hall	Sepia	Normanton Road			1913
783	Castle Donington	Cedar Tree, street scene	B/W	Market Hall			1913
784	Hulland Ward	The Hollow		Normanton Road			1913
785	Hemington	Ladies Close	B/W	Normanton Road			1913
786	Castle Donington	Hemington Lane	Sepia	Normanton Road			1913
787	Hemington	Hemington Church	Sepia	Normanton Road			1913
788	King's Mills	Priest House	Sepia	Normanton Road			1913
789	King's Mills	Chain Bridge	Sepia	Normanton Road			1913
790	Hulland Ward	The Fish Pond	B/W		White		1913
791	Hulland Ward	The Woods	B/W		White		1913
795	Biggin-by-Hulland	Village scene	B/W	Normanton Road			1913
796	Duffield	Little Eaton Bank, Stapleton's Post Office	Sepia	Stapleton's P.O.		1921	1913
797	Duffield	Eaton Hill	Sepia	Stapleton's P.O.			1913
800	Duffield	King Street	Sepia	Stapleton's P.O.			1913
801	Duffield	Hazelwood Road	Sepia	Stapleton's P.O.			1913

No	Place	Scene	Print Type	Where Published	Border Type	Date Posted	Prob Date
802	Duffield	Castle Orchard, street scene	Sepia	Normanton Road			1913
803	Duffield	Castle Orchard, street and cart	Sepia	Normanton Road			1913
804	Milford	Duffield Road, horse and cart,	Sepia	Normanton Road			1913
805	Littleover	Donkey Lane	Sepia	Normanton Road	Ornate		1913
807	Moria	Moria and Donisthorpe Institute	Sepia	Normanton Road	Ornate		1913
808	Moria	Moria canal, from Culls side		Normanton Road	Ornate		1913
809	Moria	Moria canal, 3 barges, Round House		Normanton Road	Ornate		1913
810	Moria	Moria furnace, 2 buildings		Normanton Road	Ornate		1913
812	Moria	Moria Station		Normanton Road	Ornate		1913
814	Newton Solney	Village	Sepia	Normanton Road	Ornate		1913
815	Newton Solney	The Green, street view	Sepia	Normanton Road	Ornate		1913
816	Newton Solney	The Rock and river	Sepia	Normanton Road	Ornate		1913
817	Newton Solney	River Walk and Rock	Sepia	Normanton Road	Ornate		1913
818	Newton Solney	The Rock	Sepia	Normanton Road			1913
820	Derby	Rolls-Royce	B/W	St Dunstan's P.O.	Ornate		1913
821	Derby	Rolls-Royce	B/W	St Dunstan's P.O.	Ornate		1913
823	Derby	Babington Lane, theatre and tram		Normanton Road	Ornate		1914
824	Derby	Five multi view	Sepia	Normanton Road	Pallete	1924	1914
825	Barton under Needwood	Five multi view	Sepia	Normanton Road	Pallete		1914
827	Dunstall	Dunstall Hall		Normanton Road	Ornate		1914
828	Dunstall	Dunstall Hall, The Conservatory		Normanton Road	Ornate		1914
829	Dunstall	Dunstall Hall, The Conservatory		Normanton Road	Ornate		1914
830	Woodville	Burton Road, horse and cart		Normanton Road	Ornate		1914
832	Derby	St Werburgh's Church, interior	HB/WH	Normanton Road			1914
833	Derby	St Luke's Church, interior	Sepia	Normanton Road			1914
834	Derby	St Alkmund's Church, interior		Normanton Road			1914
835	Derby	St Mary's Church, interior	Sepia	Normanton Road			1914
836	Spondon	Chapel Street Post Office		Normanton Road	Ornate	1914	1914*
838	Kirk Langley	School house	Sepia	Normanton Road	Ornate		1914
839	Kirk Langley	Church Lane and pond		Normanton Road	Ornate		1914
840	Kirk Langley	Derby Road		Normanton Road	Ornate		1914
844	Coxbench	Village scene		Normanton Road	Ornate		1914
845	Osmaston	Osmaston Manor	Sepia	Normanton Road			1914
846	Derby	St Peter's Churchyard	Sepia	Normanton Road			1914
847	Derby	Market Hall and Scarratts stall	Sepia	Normanton Road			1914
848	Derby	All Saints' Church, interior	Sepia	Normanton Road			1914
849	Derby	All Saints, the Consistory		Normanton Road			1914
850	Borrowash	Nottingham Road		Normanton Road		1916	1914
851	Borrowash	Nottingham Road		Normanton Road	Ornate		1914
852	Borrowash	Gordon Road		Normanton Road	Ornate	1915	1914
854	Borrowash	New Bridge		Normanton Road	Ornate		1914
860	Hanbury	Village Pump		Normanton Road	Ornate	1916	1914
861	Hanbury	Church	Sepia	Normanton Road	White		
862	Littleover	Grange Lodge		Normanton Road	Ornate		1914
863	Littleover	Winter Snow scene nr Post Office		Normanton Road		1914	1914
864	Littleover	Old Hall Road		Normanton Road		1914	1914
865	Littleover	The Hollow, winter snow scene		Normanton Road			1914
866	Netherseal	Post Office		E. Ford			1914
867	Derby	Fountain Arboretum		Normanton Road	Ornate	1914	1914
868	Repton	Cross and church		Normanton Road	Ornate		1914
869	Dovedale	Entrance to Dovedale	Sepia	Normanton Road			1914
870	Dovedale	The Stepping Stones		Normanton Road			1914
871	Dovedale	View		Normanton Road			1914
872	Dovedale	Tissington Spires		Normanton Road			1914
874	Barton under Needwood	The Green					1914
875	Barton under Needwood	Barton and Walton Station		Normanton Road	Ornate		1914
876	Barton under Needwood	The Hospital	B/W	Normanton Road			1914
877	Barton under Needwood	Church interior	Sepia	Normanton Road			1914
878	Barton under Needwood	Nutthall (Hall)	Sepia	Normanton Road			1914
880	Dunstall	Dunstall Hall		Normanton Road			1914
881	Dunstall	Dunstall Hall - The Farm		Normanton Road			1914
882	Dunstall	Village street scene		Normanton Road	Ornate		1914
883	Woodhouses	Lane, horses and children		Normanton Road	Ornate		1914
884	Weston-on-Trent	Street scene (farm), Little London	B/W	Normanton Road			1914
885	Weston-on-Trent	Station		Normanton Road			1914
886	Weston-on-Trent	Station	B/W	Normanton Road			1914
887	Weston-on-Trent	The Effigies, Church interior	B/W	Normanton Road			1914
888	Weston-on-Trent	The Rectory	B/W	Normanton Road			1914
889	Hanbury	Church Lane		Normanton Road	Ornate		1914
889	Weston-on-Trent	From Little London	Sepia	Normanton Road			1914
890	Weston-on-Trent	Station Corner	Sepia	Normanton Road		1915	1914

No	Place	Scene	Print Type	Where Published	Border Type	Date Posted	Prob Date
892	Derby	Five Lamps, Duffield Road, tram	Sepia	Normanton Road			1914
893	Derby	Duffield Road	Sepia	Normanton Road		1914	1914
895	Derby	Free Library	B/W (Vert)	Normanton Road			1914*
896	Derby	St John's	Sepia	Normanton Road			1914
899	Castle Donington	Key House	Sepia	Normanton Road			1914
901	Shirebrook	Central Drive	Sepia	Normanton Road			1914
903	Shirebrook	Market Place	Sepia	Normanton Road			1914
907	Shirebrook	Main Street (shops)	Sepia	Normanton Road		1914	1914
908	Chellaston	Derby Road, New Inn pub	Sepia	Normanton Road		1914	1914*
909	Chellaston	High Street (The Lawns)		Normanton Road		1914	1914*
912	Aston-on-Trent	Lodge from lake	Sepia	Normanton Road			1914
913	Aston-on-Trent	The Lodge	Sepia	Normanton Road			1914
914	Ashby-de-la-Zouch	Market Street	Sepia	Normanton Road			1914
916	Kegworth	Loughborough Road	Sepia	Normanton Road			1914
917	Kegworth	Nottingham Road	Sepia (Vert)	Normanton Road			1914
918	Kegworth	Church and Post Office	Sepia (Vert)	Normanton Road			1914
919	Kegworth	Church, interior	Sepia	Normanton Road			1914
920	Kegworth	Market Place	Sepia	Normanton Road			1914
921	Derby	Training College	Sepia	Normanton Road			1914
922	Egginton	Village (2), street scene	Sepia	Normanton Road			1914
923	Egginton	Egginton Church, interior	Sepia	Normanton Road			1914
925	Egginton	Village	B/W	Normanton Road			1914
928	Egginton	Egginton Hall	Sepia	Normanton Road			1914
929	Egginton	Egginton Hall from the lake	B/W	Normanton Road			1914
930	Alrewas	Paul Pry Inn	Sepia	Normanton Road			1914
931	Alrewas	Lychgates	Sepia	Normanton Road			1914
933	Alrewas	Burton Road	Sepia	Normanton Road			1914
934	Castle Donington	Borough Street	Sepia	Normanton Road			1914
935	Castle Donington	Wesleyan Chapel	Sepia (Vert)	Normanton Road			1914
936	Castle Donington	Donington Park Lodge	Sepia	Normanton Road			1914
937	King's Mills	Rustic Bridge	Sepia	Normanton Road			1914
938	King's Mills		Sepia	Normanton Road			1914
939	King's Mills		Sepia	Normanton Road			1914
940	Draycott	Station Road. The Lace Mill	B/W	Normanton Road		1924	1914
941	Wilne	Wilne Mill	Sepia	Normanton Road			1914
942	Wilne	Village (house and church)	B/W	Normanton Road		1917	1914
943	Breadsall	Church and Post Office	Sepia (Vert)	Normanton Road			1914
944	Breadsall	Church fire	Sepia	Normanton Road			1914
945	Breadsall	Church fire	Sepia	Normanton Road			1914
946	Hartshorne	Church	B/W	Normanton Road			1914
949	Coxbench	Derby Road	B/W	Normanton Road			1914
950	Morley	Church, porch	Sepia	Normanton Road			1914
951	Stanton-by-Bridge	Church		Normanton Road			1914
953	Kegworth	Mill Lane and cottages (same as 631)	B/W	Normanton Road			1914
954	Kegworth	Church	Sepia (Vert)	Normanton Road			1914*
955	Kegworth	Bridge	Sepia	Normanton Road			1914*
957	Kegworth	High Street	Sepia	Normanton Road			1914*
958	Aston-on-Trent	The Lodge	Sepia	Normanton Road			1914
960	Ticknall	Post Office	Sepia	Normanton Road			1914
961	Ticknall	Main Street	Sepia	Normanton Road			1914
962	Ticknall	High Street, horse and cart	Sepia	Normanton Road			1914
963	Ticknall	Church	Sepia	Normanton Road			1915
964	Hartshorne	Old Manor House and road	B/W	Normanton Road			1915
967	Breedon-on-the-Hill	Breedon Hill Church, interior	B/W	Normanton Road			1915
968	Breedon-on-the-Hill	Breedon Hill Church, exterior	Sepia	Normanton Road		1923	1915
972	Overseal	Main Street	B/W	Normanton Road			1915
974	Swarkestone	Church	Sepia	Normanton Road			1915
976	Derby	Hippodrome, Green Lane	B/W	Normanton Road		1917	1915*
977	Derby	Hippodrome	Sepia	Normanton Road			1915*
978	Derby	St Andrew's Church, interior	Sepia	Normanton Road			1915
979	Derby	St Anne's Church, interior	Sepia	Normanton Road			1915
980	Derby	Derby from the river	Sepia	Normanton Road		1916	1915*
981	Derby	Cemetery Hill, Nottingham Road	Sepia	Normanton Road		1928	1915
982	Lichfield	Cathedral	B/W	Normanton Road			1915
983	Lichfield	Cathedral	Sepia (Vert)	Normanton Road			1915
984	Lichfield	Cathedral, interior	Sepia	Normanton Road			1915
985	Lichfield	Cathedral, sleeping children	Sepia	Normanton Road			1915
986	Lichfield	Cathedral, interior	Sepia	Normanton Road	Tablet		1915
987	Lichfield	Old Mans Hospital, horse and cart	Sepia	Normanton Road			1915
988	Lichfield	Dr. Johnson's Monument	Sepia (Vert)	Normanton Road			1915
989	Lichfield	St Chad's Well	Sepia (Vert)	Normanton Road			1915

No	Place	Scene	Print Type	Where Published	Border Type	Date Posted	Prob Date
990	Wychnor	Wychnor Hall	Sepia	Normanton Road		1919	1915
991	Wychnor	Wychnor Hall	Sepia	Normanton Road			1915
995	Church Broughton			Normanton Road			1915
997	Church Broughton	Church, interior	B/W	Normanton Road			1915
998	Stanton-by-Bridge	Church		Normanton Road			1915
1002	Egginton	St Wilfrid's Church	Sepia	Normanton Road			1915
1003	Egginton	St Wilfrid's Church	Sepia	Normanton Road			1915
1005	Aston-on-Trent	Hall	Sepia	Normanton Road		1916	1915*
1006	Castle Donington	Hall and Entanglements	B/W	Normanton Road	White		1915
1008	Castle Donington	Hall, Chapel	Sepia	Normanton Road			1915
1010	Milford	Bridge and weirs from the Rock(same as 342)	Sepia	Normanton Road			1915
1011	Milford	Hopping Hill and church	Sepia	Normanton Road			1915
1012	Ockbrook	From Carr Hill	Sepia	Normanton Road		1918	1915
1013	Ockbrook	Bare Lane	Sepia	Normanton Road			1915
1014	Ockbrook	Church	Sepia (Vert)	Normanton Road			1915
1015	Ockbrook	Green Lane		Normanton Road			1915
1016	Ockbrook	Street scene	Sepia	Normanton Road			1915
1017	Ockbrook	Flood Street	Sepia	Normanton Road	White		1915
1018	Ockbrook	Lecture Hall	Sepia	Normanton Road			1915
1019	King's Mills	The Ferry (large boat)	Sepia	Normanton Road			1915
1020	Castle Donington	Hall (entanglements)	Sepia	Normanton Road			1915
1021	Castle Donington	Hall and Sentry Box	Sepia	Normanton Road			1915
1022	King's Mills	The Ferry	Sepia	Normanton Road			1915
1023	Castle Donington	Hall and Chapel	Sepia	Normanton Road			1915
1026	Ashby-de-la-Zouch	Burton Road (tram)	Sepia	Normanton Road			1915
1028	Ashby-de-la-Zouch	Wood Street (garage)	Sepia	Normanton Road			1915
1030	Ashby-de-la-Zouch	Holy Trinity Church	Sepia	Normanton Road			1915
1033	Polesworth	Nethersole Schools	Sepia	Normanton Road			1915
1035	Polesworth	Church, interior	Sepia	Normanton Road			1915
1037	Holbrook	Mellors Lane	Sepia	Normanton Road			1915
1039	Holbrook	Moor Pool Lane	Sepia	Normanton Road		1916	1915
1040	Holbrook	Moor	Sepia	Normanton Road			1915
1041	Holbrook	Moor, street scene	Sepia	Normanton Road		1918	1915
1042	Idridgehay	Ecclesburn (*sic*) Lane	Sepia	Normanton Road			1916
1043	Ireton Wood	The Lake	Sepia	Normanton Road			1916
1044	Idridgehay	Ecclesburn (*sic*) House	Sepia	Normanton Road			1916
1045	Idridgehay	Post Office	Sepia	Normanton Road			1916
1046	Idridgehay	Scenic view	Sepia	Normanton Road			1916
1047	Idridgehay	Derby Road	Sepia	Normanton Road			1916
1049	Little Eaton	View from bridge	Sepia	Normanton Road			1916
1050	Holbrook	Nether Lea	Sepia	Normanton Road			1916
1050	Holbrook	Coxbench Lane	Sepia	Normanton Road			1916
1051	Holbrook	Nether Lea	Sepia	Normanton Road			1916
1052	Littleover	The Hollow		Normanton Road		1927	1916
1053	Kilburn	Bywell Lane (bikes)	B/W				1916
1054	Littleover	The Hollow (bikes)	B/W		White	1920	1916
1055	Littleover	The Hollow, cottage (same as 370)	Sepia	Market Hall			1909
1056	Littleover	The Hollow, well and motor bikes		Normanton Road		1916	1916*
1057	Littleover	Entrance to	Sepia				1916
1058	Derby	Burton Road	Sepia	Market Hall			1916
1060	Derby	St James's Street	Sepia	Normanton Road			1916
1061	Derby	London Road (same as 708)	Sepia	Normanton Road		1918	1912
1062	Mayfield	Church		Market Hall			1916
1064	Mayfield	Sunny Side Guest House					1916
1065	Mayfield	Holme Bank	Sepia				1916
1068	Barrow upon Soar	War Cross	Sepia				1916
1070	Barton under Needwood	From the church (H.Simons)		H.Simons Stores		1920	1916
1071	Barton under Needwood	Aerial view (H.Simons Vic Stores)	Sepia	H.Simons Stores		1920	1916
1072	Polesworth	Market Street	Sepia				1916
1074	Polesworth	Old Nunnery Dungeons	Sepia				1916
1076	Morley	The Cross (4 variations)	Sepia	Normanton Road		1917	1916
1078	Repton	Cross and church	B/W				1917
1079	Repton	Burton Road, horse and cart	Sepia			1917	1917*
1083	Kilburn	Church Street	B/W				1917
1084	Egginton	Multi view			Pallete		1917
1100	Rocester	Rocester Mill, Churnet bridge and weir	Sepia				1917
1101	Rocester	On the River Dove					1917
1102	Barton under Needwood	Church	Sepia				1917
1105	Derby	Multi view					1917
1107	Sutton Bonnington	Five multi view			Pallete		1917
1109	Derby	Florence Nightingate statue (Lilywhite Ltd)	B/W				1917

No	Place	Scene	Print Type	Where Published	Border Type	Date Posted	Prob Date
1115	Ockbrook	Green Lane				1918	1918*
1118	Lichfield	St Mary's Church					1920
1127	Lichfield	The Recreation Ground					1920
1130	Barton under Needwood	War Memorial and church	B/W				1920
1132	Burton upon Trent	War Memorial	Sepia				1920
1133	Burton upon Trent	Cherry Orchard	B/W				1920
1134	Burton upon Trent	Ox Hay, bridge, children	B/W				1920
1135	Burton upon Trent	Stapenhill Church from the Ox Hay	B/W		White	1928	1920
1136	Stapenhill	Church					1920
1142	Mickleover	Thatched Cottage, Straker Lane	B/W				1920
1145	Littleover	Church Street	B/W				1920
1146	Littleover	Chain Lane	B/W			1924	1924*
1149	King's Mills	Weir	Sepia		White		1924
1150	Breadsall	Brookside	Sepia		White	1928	1924
1151	Breadsall	Cows	Sepia		White		1924
1152	Breadsall	Church	B/W (Vert)		White		1924
1153	Breadsall	Corner shop	Sepia	Market Hall		1928	1924
1154	Breadsall	Thatched Cottage	Sepia	Market Hall	White		1924
1158	Willington	Trent Bridge	B/W	Market Hall			1924
1160	Alvaston	Alvaston Lake	Sepia	Market Hall	White		1924
1162	Alvaston	Lake and Pavilion		Market Hall			1924
1163	Alvaston	Lake and Pavilion	B/W	Market Hall			1924
1164	Ashby-de-la-Zouch	Castle	Sepia (Vert)		White		1924
1165	Ashby-de-la-Zouch	The Doorway of Banqueting Hall at Castle	Sepia		White		1924
1166	Ashby-de-la-Zouch	Castle, Kitchen Tower	Sepia (Vert)		White		1924
1167	Ashby-de-la-Zouch	Castle, Queen Marys room					1924
1168	Ashby-de-la-Zouch	Castle	Sepia	George Brown	White		1924
1169	Ashby-de-la-Zouch	Castle	Sepia	George Brown	White		1933
1170	Ashby-de-la-Zouch	Castle	Sepia		White		1924
1171	Ashby-de-la-Zouch	Manor House and The Castle	B/W				1924
1172	Ashby-de-la-Zouch	Manor House					1924
1173	Ashby-de-la-Zouch	Parish Church, Huntingdon Tomb	Sepia		White		1924
1174	Ashby-de-la-Zouch	St Helen's Church	Sepia		White		1924
1176	Ashby-de-la-Zouch	County Cricket Ground	Sepia		White		1924
1177	Ashby-de-la-Zouch	Loudon Memorial	Sepia (Vert)		White		1924
1178	Ashby-de-la-Zouch	Willesley Road	Sepia		White		1924
1179	Ashby-de-la-Zouch	Entrance to Lord Hastings Tower at Castle	Sepia				1924
1180	Derby	Bus Terminus, Cheapside	Sepia	Market Hall		1927	1925
1181	Derby	Market Place, War Memorial	Sepia	Market Hall			1925*
1183	Repton	Derby Road	Sepia	Market Hall			1925
1185	Ashby-de-la-Zouch	Market Street	Sepia	Market Hall			1925
1186	Winshill	Mill Hill Lane	Sepia	Market Hall			1925
1189	Old Winshill	The Brook		Market Hall			1925
1191	Aston-on-Trent	Church and Lychgates	Sepia	Market Hall			1925
1192	Borrowash	Victoria Road	Sepia	Market Hall			1925
1195	Kingston on Soar	Church and Lychgates	B/W	Market Hall			1925
1196	Borrowash	Derby Road	Sepia	Market Hall			1925
1197	Borrowash	Nottingham Road	Sepia	Market Hall			1925
1198	Kingston-on-Soar	Church and Lychgates		Market Hall			1925
1199	Kingston-on-Soar	Church, interior	Sepia	Market Hall			1925
1200	Kingston-on-Soar	Village pump	Sepia	Market Hall			1925
1201	Weston-on-Trent	Church doorway	Sepia	Market Hall			1925
1203	King's Mills	Chain Bridge	B/W	Market Hall			1925
1204	Chaddesden	Church	Sepia	Market Hall			1925
1205	Mayfield	The Hall	Sepia	Market Hall			1925
1206	Quarndon	Old Church (same as 661)	Sepia (Vert)	Market Hall		1927	1912
1209	Dunstall	Hall	Sepia	Market Hall	White		1925
1211	Youlgreave	Main Street	Sepia	Market Hall	White	1926	1925
1213	Bradford Dale	River and trees	Sepia	Market Hall			1925
1215	Castle Donington	The Cross, Donington Park	Sepia	Market Hall			1925
1217	Wirksworth	Pulpit, Free Church interior (Dinah Morris)	Sepia	Market Hall		1926	1925
1218	Mayfield	Spring Cottage and Corn Mill	Sepia (Vert)	Market Hall			1925
1235	Derby	Chester Green (swings)	Sepia	Market Hall			1925
1238	Moria	The Old Furnace	Sepia	Market Hall			1925
1249	Hulland Ward	Church	B/W	Market Hall			1925
1250	Hulland Ward	Derby Road	Sepia	Market Hall	White	1928	1925
1254	Derby	Little Nymphs, Derwent Park	Sepia	Market Hall			1925
1255	Derby	Walk, Derwent Park	Sepia	Market Hall			1925
1257	Derby	Bonny Face in Derwent Park		Market Hall		1929	1925
1258	Alvaston	Approach to Lake		Market Hall		1926	1925*
1260	Alvaston	Alvaston Lake, landing stage	Sepia	Market Hall			1925*

No	Place	Scene	Print Type	Where Published	Border Type	Date Posted	Prob Date
1261	Alvaston	Alvaston Lake from the landing stage	Sepia	Market Hall			1925*
1274	Wirksworth	Steeple Grange (car)	Sepia	Market Hall		1926	1925
1275	Wirksworth	Lower end (car)	Sepia	Market Hall			1925
1276	Wirksworth	Cromford Road	Sepia	Market Hall			1925
1277	Hanbury	Church Lane		Market Hall	White	1928	1925
1278	Draycott	Howell Road (car)	Sepia	Market Hall			1925
1279	Draycott	Street scene (shop)	Sepia	Market Hall		1927	1925
1282	Elvaston	Castle		Market Hall			1925
1283	Elvaston	Castle, east front	Sepia	Market Hall			1925
1284	Elvaston	Castle, end lake	Sepia	Market Hall			1925
1285	Elvaston	Castle grounds, rockery	Sepia	Market Hall			1925
1287	Elvaston	Italian Gardens	Sepia	Green Lane			1925
1288	Elvaston	Castle					1925
1290	Castle Donington	The Windmill	Sepia	Market Hall			1926
1291	Mayfield	Hanging Bridge	Sepia	Market Hall			1926
1292	Long Whatton	The Church	Sepia	Market Hall			1926
1293	Long Whatton	Street scene and car	Sepia	Market Hall			1926
1296	Borrowash	Fountain Nurseries	Sepia	Market Hall			1926
1299	Melbourne	The weirs (from lake)	Sepia	Market Hall			1926
1300	Ashby-de-la-Zouch	Castle	Sepia	Market Hall	White		1926
1301	Ashby-de-la-Zouch	Tamworth Road	Sepia	Market Hall	White		1926
1302	Ockbrook	Church and street scene	Sepia	Market Hall			1926
1303	Ockbrook	The Church, Morovain settlement	Sepia	Market Hall			1926
1305	Kingston-on-Soar	Church and pump	Sepia	Market Hall			1926
1308	Derby	War Memorial, Market Place	Sepia	Market Hall			1927
1311	Derby	St Michael's Church		Market Hall			1927
1316	Derby	Chester Green (park)	Sepia	Market Hall			1927
1318	Derby	St Mary's Bridge (man cycling)	Sepia	Market Hall		1932	1927
1319	Derby	St Paul's Church	Sepia	Market Hall			1927
1323	Derby	Hill Brow, Stenson Road	Sepia	Market Hall			1927
1330	Derby	King Street	Sepia	Market Hall			1927
1332	Burton upon Trent	War Memorial	Sepia	Market Hall			1927
1333	Derby	All Saints Church	Sepia	Market Hall			1927
1334	Derby	New Uttoxeter Road (dog and car)	Sepia	Market Hall			1927
1335	Derby	LMS Cenotaph, Station Street		Market Hall		1927	1927*
1338	Burton upon Trent	Trent Bridge and dog	Sepia	Market Hall			1927
1339	Newton Solney	Hill Top Lane	B/W	Market Hall			1927
1340	Stapenhill	St Peter's Street (car)	Sepia	Market Hall			1927
1341	Stapenhill	Mystic Castle, riverside	Sepia	Market Hall			1927
1342	Burton upon Trent	Newton Road	Sepia	Market Hall			1927
1345	King's Mills	The Cottages (car)	Sepia	Market Hall			1927
1348	Ticknall	Main Street	Sepia	Market Hall			1927
1350	Ticknall	The Arch	Sepia	Market Hall			1927
1353	Lichfield	St Chad's Church	Sepia	Market Hall			1927
1357	Derby	Derby China, The Dances	Sepia (Vert)	Market Hall			1928
1358	Derby	Derby China, Jug	Sepia	Market Hall			1928
1359	Derby	Derby China, (Thistle Dish)	Sepia	Market Hall			1928
1360	Derby	Derby China, Prentice Plate by W.M.Billingsley	Sepia	Market Hall			1928
1365	Ticknall	Church, interior	B/W	Market Hall	White	1939	1928
1366	Swarkestone	Trent and bridge	B/W	Market Hall			1928
1367	Swarkestone	Bridge	Sepia	Market Hall			1928
1369	Long Whatton	Street scene (Royal Oak)	Sepia	Market Hall			1928
1372	Alrewas	Interior of church		Market Hall			1928
1375	Alrewas	Park Road	Sepia	Market Hall			1928
1378	Derby	King's Hall	Sepia	Market Hall			1928
1379	Derby	King's Hall	Sepia	Market Hall			1928
1380	Derby	King's Hall	Sepia	Market Hall			1928
1381	King's Mills	The Ferry Boat	Sepia	Market Hall			1928
1383	Ashby-de-la-Zouch	Parish church, interior	Sepia	Market Hall			1928
1384	Ashby-de-la-Zouch	Five multi view	Sepia	Market Hall			1928
1385	Staunton Harold	Hall and church	Sepia	Market Hall			1928
1386	Derby	Multi view	B/W	Market Hall			1928
1389	Derby	Multi view (x 3 vertical)	B/W	Market Hall			1928
1391	Chaddesden	Chaddesden, Derby	B/W	Market Hall	White	1929	1928*
1394	Ashby-de-la-Zouch	Grammar School	Sepia	Market Hall			1929
1395	Ashby-de-la-Zouch	Elizabethan Building	Sepia	Market Hall			1929
1397	Stapenhill	Recreation and dog	Sepia	Market Hall			1929
1399	Burton upon Trent	Bridge and shelter	Sepia	Market Hall			1929
1406	Repton	Church and Lynchgates		Market Hall			1929
1408	Barrow upon Trent	The Hall	Sepia	Market Hall			1929
1409	Barrow upon Trent	Village scene	Sepia	Market Hall			1929

No	Place	Scene	Print Type	Where Published	Border Type	Date Posted	Prob Date
1410	Derby	The Free Library and Museum		Market Hall			1929
1411	Derby	Wardwick	Sepia	Market Hall			1930
1412	Derby	Uttoxeter New Road	Sepia	Market Hall			1930
1413	Swarkestone	River Trent	Sepia	Market Hall			1930
1414	Swarkestone	Wood Shop and bridge	Sepia	Market Hall			1930
1415	Swarkestone	The Yard Lane	Sepia	Market Hall		1931	1930
1416	Swarkestone	The Hall	Sepia	Market Hall			1930
1417	Swarkestone	The Hall	Sepia	Market Hall			1930
1418	Snelston			Market Hall			1930
1419	Snelston	Village	Sepia	Market Hall			1930
1422	Tissington	The Avenue	Sepia	Market Hall			1930
1424	Tissington	School and pond	Sepia	Market Hall			1930
1425	Tissington	Town and pond	Sepia	Market Hall			1930
1429	Clifton	War Memorial	Sepia	Market Hall			1930
1436	Little Eaton	The Church	Sepia	Market Hall			1930
1450	Ambergate	Oakhurst (house)	Sepia	Market Hall			1930
1451	Ambergate	Oakhurst, showing Chapel	Sepia	Market Hall			1930
1452	Ambergate	Oakhurst	Sepia	Market Hall			1930
1453	Ambergate	The Village, Hill view, station	B/W	Market Hall			1930
1454	Ambergate	Post Office	Sepia	Market Hall		1938	1930
1456	Ambergate	The Church	Sepia	Market Hall			1930
1457	Ambergate	Church, interior	Sepia	Market Hall			1930
1458	Ambergate	Railway Station	Sepia	Market Hall			1930
1459	Ambergate	Matlock Road, Hurt Arms	Sepia	Market Hall		1932	1930
1460	Ambergate	Main Street	Sepia	Market Hall			1930
1461	Diseworth	Hall Gate (1)	Sepia	Market Hall			1930
1462	Diseworth	Hall Gate (2)	Sepia	Market Hall			1930
1463	Diseworth	The Church	Sepia	Market Hall			1930
1464	Diseworth	Hall Gate (3), street scene	Sepia	Market Hall			1930
1465	Diseworth	Church Street		Market Hall			1930
1467	Diseworth	Town End	Sepia	Market Hall			1930
1468	Diseworth	Church, interior	Sepia	Market Hall	White		1930
1469	Alrewas	All Saints Church		Market Hall	White		1930
1470	Alrewas	The Gallows Bridge	B/W	Market Hall			1930
1471	Alrewas	Main Street	Sepia	Market Hall			1930
1472	Alrewas	Mill Waterfall		Market Hall			1930
1473	Alrewas	The Square	Sepia	Market Hall	White		1930
1474	Barton under Needwood	Main Street		Market Hall			1930
1477	Barton under Needwood	Main Street	Sepia	Market Hall	White		1930
1480	Alvaston	Alvaston Terminus	Sepia	Market Hall			1931
1482	Alvaston	Carnegie Library	Sepia	Market Hall			1931
1483	Alvaston	London Road from Alvaston Terminus	Sepia	Market Hall			1931
1484	Alvaston	Toll Gate, London Road	Sepia	Market Hall			1931
1485	Alvaston	Shardlow Road	Sepia	Market Hall			1931
1486	Alvaston	Alvaston Street	Sepia	Market Hall			1931
1487	Alvaston	The Green	Sepia	Market Hall			1931
1488	Derby	London Road, Alvaston	Sepia	Market Hall			1931
1489	Derby	Belper Road		Market Hall			1931
1492	Hanbury	The School		Market Hall			1931
1493	Hanbury	Martins Lane	Sepia	Market Hall			1931
1496	Burton upon Trent	Christ Church, New Street	B/W	Market Hall			1931
1497	Burton upon Trent	War Memorial and High Street		Market Hall			1931
1499	Ockbrook	Church		Market Hall	Oval		1931
1500	Ockbrook	From Carr Hill		Market Hall	Oval		1931
1501	Lockington	Lodge and church	B/W	Market Hall			1931
1504	King's Mills	Ferry Road	B/W	Market Hall			1931
1506	King's Mills	Ferry Road	B/W	Market Hall			1931
1507	Hemington	Street scene	B/W	Market Hall			1931
1509	Diseworth	Grimes Gate	B/W	Market Hall			1931
1528	Ashby-de-la-Zouch	Church, Lady of Lourdes (street scene)	Sepia	Market Hall			1931
1531	Snarestone	Globe Inn, Main Street	Sepia	Market Hall			1931
1532	Snarestone	Main Street, Thatched Cottages	Sepia	Market Hall			1931
1536	Snarestone	The Memorial		Market Hall			1931
1537	Castle Donington	Hall with deer	Sepia	Market Hall			1931
1538	Repton	Church and Lychgates	Sepia	Market Hall			1932
1539	Repton	Mill	Sepia	Market Hall			1932
1540	Repton	Cross and church	Sepia	Market Hall			1932
1541	Repton	Post Office	Sepia	Market Hall			1932
1542	Littleover	Shepherd Street and pub	Sepia	Market Hall		1939	1932
1543	Littleover	Normanton Lane	Sepia	Market Hall			1932
1547	Chellaston	St Peter's Church		Market Hall			1932

No	Place	Scene	Print Type	Where Published	Border Type	Date Posted	Prob Date
1548	Chellaston	High Street from Church Tower	Sepia	Market Hall			1932
1549	Chellaston	High Street (Raynes shop)	Sepia	Market Hall		1932	1932*
1551	Burton upon Trent	Waterloo Street		Market Hall			1932
1553	Burton upon Trent	Pirelli Tyre works	Sepia	Market Hall			1932
1554	Burton upon Trent	Pirelli Tyre works	Sepia	Market Hall			1932
1556	Burton upon Trent	Horninglow Church	Sepia (Vert)	Market Hall			1932
1557	Burton upon Trent	Borough Road	Sepia	Market Hall			1932
1569	Ambergate	Canal from long tunnel	Sepia	Market Hall			1932
1573	Ashby-de-la-Zouch	Parish Church		Market Hall			1932
1574	Breedon-on-the-Hill	Church	Sepia	Market Hall			1932
1575	Breedon-on-the-Hill	War Memorial		Market Hall			1932
1576	Derby	Exeter Bridge, Derwent Street		Market Hall		1938	1932*
1580	Stapenhill	Feeding swans	Sepia	Market Hall			1932
1581	Stapenhill	Riverside walk	Sepia	Market Hall			1932
1583	Stapenhill	Riverside Lawn, Burton upon Trent		Market Hall			1932
1585	Burton upon Trent	View from Trent Bridge	Sepia	Market Hall			1932
1586	Derby	Floods 22 May 1932, Bus in Wardwick	Sepia	Market Hall			1932*
1587	Derby	Floods 22 May 1932, Sadler Gate	Sepia	Market Hall			1932*
1588	Swarkestone	Church (across fields)	Sepia	Market Hall			1933
1590	Newhall	The Church		Market Hall			1933
1591	Stapenhill	Riverside Walk	Sepia	Market Hall			1933
1595	Newhall	Sunnyside, looking down	Sepia	Market Hall			1933
1596	Newhall	Rambling in spinney	Sepia	Market Hall			1933
1597	Moria	Ashby Road	Sepia	Market Hall			1933
1598	Moria	Canal and bridge	Sepia	Market Hall			1933
1600	Moria	Station interior	Sepia	Market Hall			1933
1603	Donisthorpe	Memorial Gates and Lychgates	Sepia	Market Hall			1933
1604	Moria	Relection, The Furnace	Sepia	Market Hall			1933
1605	Kingston-on-Soar	Kingston Hall - Natures Mirror, The lake	Sepia	Market Hall			1933
1612	Youlgrave	Ravenstor Rock	Sepia	Market Hall			1933
1614	Ockbrook	Bare House Lane	Sepia	Market Hall			1933
1615	Ockbrook	Church Street	Sepia	Market Hall			1933
1618	Ockbrook	The Riddings		Market Hall			1933
1623	Kegworth	Bridge and River Soar		Market Hall			1934
1624	Kegworth	Footbridge and River Soar	Sepia	Market Hall			1934
1625	Tutbury	Multi view		Market Hall	Pallete		1934
1627	Ashby-de-la-Zouch	Elizabethan Building, Market Street		Market Hall			1934
1628	Etwall	St Helen's Church	Sepia	Market Hall			1934
1630	Etwall	Isolation Hospital	Sepia	Market Hall			1934
1631	Etwall	Etwall Hall	Sepia	Market Hall			1934
1632	Etwall	Main Street, from the Green	Sepia	Market Hall			1934
1636	Stapenhill	Pleasure Ground	Sepia	Market Hall			1934
1637	Etwall	The Almshouses		Market Hall			1934
1639	Tutbury	Castle	Sepia (Vert)	Market Hall			1934
1640	Tutbury	Castle, High Tower	Sepia	Market Hall			1934
1641	Tutbury	Memorial Chapel	Sepia	Market Hall	White		1934
1644	Breedon-on-the-Hill	Round House	Sepia	Market Hall			1934
1646	Kegworth	Flying Horse Hotel	Sepia	Market Hall			1934
1647	Denstone	Heywood Memorial		Market Hall			1934
1652	Osmaston	Pond view	Sepia	Market Hall			1934
1653	Osmaston	Cottages and pump	Sepia	Market Hall			1934
1657	Breedon-on-the-Hill	War Memorial	Sepia	Market Hall			1934
1659	Worthington	Village		Market Hall			1934
1663	Derby	River Gardens, Peter Pan	Sepia	Market Hall			1935
1665	Derby	Exeter Bridge	B/W	Market Hall			1935
1667	Derby	The Moreledge, street scene	Sepia	Market Hall			1935
1668	Derby	Corn Market, bus and cart	Sepia	Market Hall			1935
1670	Derby	Bus Station (Harts the Chemist)	Sepia	Market Hall		1936	1935
1671	Derby	St Peter's Street	Sepia	Market Hall			1935
1674	Derby	Jubliee Decorations (1935) Market Place	Sepia	Market Hall		1935	1935*
1676	Derby	Arboretum, Memorial and fountain	Sepia	Market Hall			1935
1678	Derby	Arboretum, The Boar	Sepia	Market Hall			1935
1681	Derby	River, Derwent Park	Sepia	Market Hall			1935
1683	Derby	Riverside Garden	Sepia	Market Hall			1935
1684	Derby	Victoria Street and Post Office	Sepia	Market Hall		1935	1935*
1686	Darley Dale	Boating Lake, Whitworth Institute	Sepia	Market Hall		1937	1936
1688	Darley Bridge	Post Office and street scene	Sepia	Market Hall			1936
1689	Darley Bridge	Post Office	Sepia	Market Hall			1936
1692	Barton Under Needwood	Old Cottages		Market Hall			1936
1695	Barton Under Needwood	Main Street	Sepia	Market Hall			1936
1697	Willesley	Golf House and course	Sepia	Market Hall			1936

No	Place	Scene	Print Type	Where Published	Border Type	Date Posted	Prob Date
1699	Ashby-de-la-Zouch	The Hill, Hill Street	Sepia	Market Hall			1936
1703	Cheddleton	Village, street scene	Sepia	Market Hall			1936
1706	Matlock	The Boating lake	Sepia	Market Hall			1936
1710	Derby	Dahlias, River Gardens	Sepia	Market Hall		1936	1936
1712	Derby	Lily Pond, River Gardens	Sepia	Market Hall			1936*
1716	Alvaston	Alvaston Lake, Formation swimming		Market Hall			1936*
1718	Markeaton	The Lake, the swans	Sepia	Market Hall			1936
1721	Derby	Town Hall, illumination		Market Hall			1936
1725	Hulland Ward	Post Office		Market Hall			1936
1726	Hulland Ward	Wardgate		Market Hall		1937	1936
1728	Barton under Needwood	Church and Memorial	Sepia	Market Hall			1936
1730	Castle Donington	Five multi view	Sepia	Market Hall		1938	1936
1733	Measham	Church		Market Hall			1936
1734	Borrowash	Derby Road (lorry)	Sepia	Market Hall		1939	1936
1735	Borrowash	The Nurseries	Sepia	Market Hall		1937	1936*
1738	Tonge	Village, street scene	Sepia	Market Hall			1936
1739	Sheepy	River, scene and pub	Sepia	Market Hall			1936
1741	Breedon-on-the-Hill	Village view from the Hill	Sepia	Market Hall			1936
1743	Turnditch	The School		Market Hall	White		1936
1748	Lockington	Bamfit Lane		Market Hall			1936
1749	Hulme End	Cawlow Farm		Market Hall			1936
1761	Sutton Bonnington	Midland Agricultural College	Sepia	Market Hall			1936
1762	Sutton Bonnington	Midland Agricultural College	Sepia	Market Hall			1936
1766	Tutbury	General view		Market Hall			1936
1768	Tutbury	Burton Street		Market Hall	White		1936
1769	Tutbury	Castle, Mary Queen of Scots Tower	Sepia	Market Hall			1936
1770	Tutbury	Castle, High Tower		Market Hall			1936
1771	Tutbury	High Street	Sepia	Market Hall			1936
1775	Idridgehay	Hillcliffe Lane and stream	Sepia	Market Hall		1937	1936/37*
1777	Tutbury	Dog and Partridge Hotel		Market Hall			1936/37
1791	Kegworth	River Soar and New Bridge	Sepia	Market Hall			1936/37
1792	Kegworth	The weir	Sepia	Market Hall			1936/37
1794	Derby	The Buck in the Park, Arboretum	Sepia	Market Hall			1936/37
1797	Ashby-de-la-Zouch	Market Street	Sepia	Market Hall			1936/37
1798	Ashby-de-la-Zouch	Market Street	Sepia	Market Hall			1936/37
1804	Derby	The new Traffic Street, opening	Sepia	Market Hall		1938	1937/38*
1807	King's Mills	Rustic Bridge and Priest House	Sepia	Market Hall			1937/38
1808	King's Mills	Old Chapel and river	Sepia	Market Hall			1937/38
1809	Castle Donington	Key House	Sepia	Market Hall			1937/38
1810	Ashby-de-la-Zouch	Hill Street		Market Hall			1937/38
1812	Alstonefield	Church	Sepia	Market Hall			1937/38
1813	Alstonefield	The Green	Sepia	Market Hall			1937/38
1815	Hope Dale	Watts Russell Inn	Sepia	Market Hall			1937/38
1816	Mill Dale	Lane Brook House	Sepia	Market Hall			1937/38
1818	Alstonefield	Church, interior	Sepia	Market Hall		1941	1937/38
1823	Derby	River Gardens, steps and bridge	Sepia	Market Hall			1937/38
1825	Tutbury	Five multi view	Sepia	Market Hall	Palette	1948	1938
1826	Tutbury	The Castle, Keep and Well		Market Hall			1938
1827	Etwall	Main Street	Sepia	Market Hall			1938
1828	Etwall	Village from Church Tower	Sepia	Market Hall			1938
1830	Etwall	Almshouses	Sepia	Market Hall			1938
1831	Kegworth	Post Office	Sepia	Market Hall			1938
1833	Sutton Bonnington	The Green	Sepia	Market Hall			1938
1834	Sutton Bonnington	Marl Pit Hill		Market Hall			1938
1835	Sutton Bonnington	St Anne's Church	Sepia	Market Hall			1938
1836	Sutton Bonnington	Hungary Lane	Sepia	Market Hall			1938
1837	Etwall	Derby Road from Church Tower	Sepia	Market Hall			1938
1840	Derby	Cornmarket		Market Hall			1938
1842	Walton-on-Trent	School and Corner		Market Hall			1938
1845	Sutton Bonnington	St Michael's Church	Sepia (Vert)	Market Hall			1938
1846	Wirksworth	Station interior and wagons	Sepia	Market Hall			1938